Welcome to the Big Sur.

We want to know you and share the home and be friends, not for just a quick weekend between San Simeon and Carmel, but for the years to come when you'll return again, loving this coast more and more as you learn its easy pace and dramatic land and seascapes.

We don't want to sell you the hills or the water or the rare sky as souvenirs, we just hope you'll take something and give something, cherishing this fragile and profound place as if it were a gold wedding band belonging to you.

The Big Sur needs knowing, needs caring, needs enduring lovers more than just a pat on the head and a quick goodbye. Every person is a visitor here — for a longer or shorter time — but the land is eternal.

Welcome, stay awhile, and please come again.

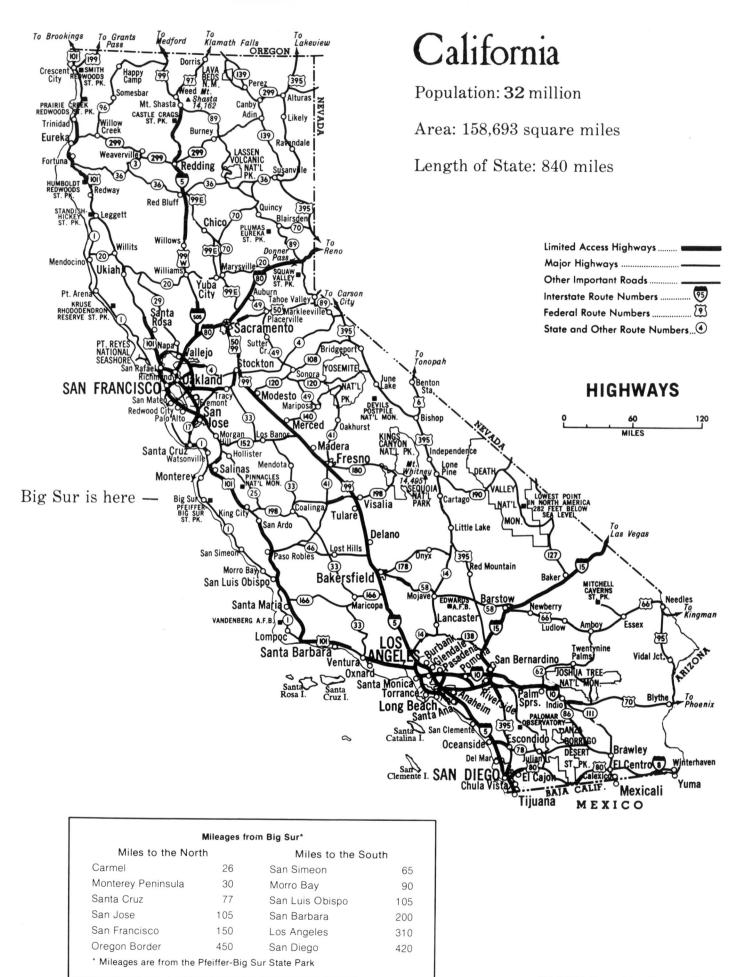

California

Population: **32** million

Area: 158,693 square miles

Length of State: 840 miles

Limited Access Highways	▬▬▬
Major Highways	━━━
Other Important Roads	━━
Interstate Route Numbers	95
Federal Route Numbers	9
State and Other Route Numbers	4

HIGHWAYS

Big Sur is here —

Mileages from Big Sur*			
Miles to the North		**Miles to the South**	
Carmel	26	San Simeon	65
Monterey Peninsula	30	Morro Bay	90
Santa Cruz	77	San Luis Obispo	105
San Jose	105	San Barbara	200
San Francisco	150	Los Angeles	310
Oregon Border	450	San Diego	420
* Mileages are from the Pfeiffer-Big Sur State Park			

Map Courtesy Hammond, Inc., Maplewood, New Jersey

Table of Contents

BIG SUR

*Original Serigraph by
Chuck Moran. This 18"x24"
print "Big Sur" is available
from Big Sur Publications,
P.O. Box 340, Big Sur, CA
93920. The price of $12.00
includes all handling costs.*

The natural grandeur of this land and seascape looking south from Rocky Point has made it a favorite subject of artists and photographers. Bixby Point, a prolongation of Long Ridge, and Hurricane Point jut into the ocean in the background. In the center of the photograph Rocky Creek runs into the ocean under one of many graceful arch span bridges along the coast. From 1898 to 1907 the green meadow near the foreground was the site of a small village called Notley's Landing where the milling and shipping of various types of lumber was carried on. (Photo by John Osterman)

BIG SUR ❧

The Story Behind the Place

Big Sur is an oasis in a hurried world. The virgin quality of the landscape, gives us a sense of our own creation. Those who come here find the realities possessing their minds to be quite different than those left behind. With its unspoiled natural charm and slow paced country life, Big Sur is reminiscent of an earlier California.

The exquisitely fashioned coastline seems too fragile to exist among such obvious forces. Mountains rise vertically from the sea. The rugged shoreline imparts granite cliffs, grassy promontories and rocky beaches. Cattle graze on hillsides flecked with wildflowers and native trees. Hawks soar in redwood canyons where gentle mountain streams flow lazily to the sea.

Big Sur stretches for ninety miles in a north-south direction along the first set of mountain ridges which surface from the sea to 3,500 feet. Most of the population, business and activity are scattered about the Big Sur Valley and its coastal outskirts.

Highway 1, the only road through the area, provides the most effective way to see Big Sur. The two lane ribbon of road winds along the crooked western edge of the Santa Lucia Mountains, climbing at times to a soaring 1,000 feet above the sea. It traverses a canyon floor, then snakes upward again, tracing the receding forms in the contoured landscape.

Big Sur's northern coast extends from south of Carmel for over twenty miles to the Big Sur Valley. The road travels one to two miles inland, flanked on the west by the river and a ridge which separates it from the coastline.

The six mile long valley is the closest thing to the center of town, although there *is* no official town. The rural community's village exists as a succession of rustic inns and lodges, post office, health center, grammar school and Grange hall. At the valley's southern end, Coast Highway 1 ascends the long, steep grade of Post Hill. Just beyond its crest, the less populated and more remote southern coast stretches sixty miles to San Simeon and the Hearst Castle.

Most people gain a sense of the length of Big Sur which Highway 1 travels. Few, however, can identify with its width since the Santa Lucia Mountains to the east are generally unapproachable by car.

The overall area covers some 300 square miles, about 192,000 acres. The federal government owns most of this undeveloped mountain region as the northern section of the Los Padres National Forest. California State Parks occupy some of the land. Only a small portion, about 58,000 acres is held in private ownership. Most of this borders the highway on the northern coast and valley region.

The early Spanish settlers to California are responsible for Big Sur's unusual name. In the early 1770's, they marched up the coast from Mexico, constructing forts and Catholic missions at strategic locations. The Carmel Mission's Spaniards referred to this forbidding wilderness to their south as *el pais grande del sur,* the big country to the south. The two rivers of the coast were named *el rio grande del sur,* the big river to the south; and *el rio chiquito del sur,* the little river to the south. The bilingual name evolved and in the early 1900's, residents petitioned the government to officially call the post office Big Sur. The correct pronunciation of *sur* sounds like a softly spoken *suwehr.*

Highway One is one of the world's most scenic. Each new crook in the road introduces unanticipated, sweeping views. The mountains, green in winter and straw colored in the summer, are known locally as the Big Sur Hills.

Occasionally, private, dirt roads wind off the highway to a cabin, probably hidden from view. One may pass an old farmhouse. On the hillsides from which the highway was carved, one sees evidence of erosion caused by heavy winter rains. In places, the eroded hills have left barbed wire fences hanging from the mountain. Bridges span wide canyons and creeks. The hills loom so large that one feels like a pocket-sized Lilliputian in a land of giants.

About 1200 people live in Big Sur. More than 800 of these reside in the valley and on the northern coast. The south coast is less inhabited because of its physical isolation.

Big Sur, isolated by its steep mountains, inaccessible shoreline and only one road in and out insures that residents live uncomplicated lives. Locals acquire a penchant for approaching life at a more leisurely pace. Most thrive on the solitude which accompanies daily life. The private dirt roads leading to many homes facilitate the quiet lifestyle.

Banks, shopping centers and movie theatres are nonexistent. Until the early 1980's, residents did not get television reception and many still choose to live without it.

Residents go to "town"—the Monterey Peninsula—for shopping, business and entertainment. Most spend at least one entire day each week there. It takes a well organized person to exist comfortably in Big Sur.

Locals always encounter friends and neighbors at the post office beside the Big Sur Center Deli and Bazaar. The rustic lodges serve as meeting places for the locals and the River Inn encourages community participation in its events such as the weekly poetry readings. Like any other community, locals entertain and socialize at individual homes.

The Captain Cooper Grammer School sits atop a mountain in the valley. Middle and high school students travel over seventy round trip miles a day to school, usually by bus. The children of the south coast attend school, at Pacific Valley, 30 miles south of the valley.

Traffic lights, neon signs and bright lights are nonexistent. Telephones and electricity did not make it to Big Sur until the early 1950's. Some south coast residents still live without electricity and telephones. Even some of the more remote north coast and valley ridges are without telephone and power lines.

The oldest residents descend from some of the original homesteaders who settled in the

1860's and thereafter. The Post, Pfeiffer-Ewoldsen, Trotter and Harlan families fit into this category. Other long time residents include a number of retired people, and others who simply came here years ago, loved the country and decided to make it home. For decades, artists and writers, preoccupied with emotion and imagination have found inspiration in the pure mountain and sea air.

A number of resort employees, forest service and state park personnel comprise a large portion of the population. Professional people maintain second homes with aspirations of full time living.

The 600 homes of Big Sur conform only to the lay of the land, which often dictates the design. From the coast highway one sees a seemingly inaccessible house perched high on the crest of an eastern ridge. Looking west, a cliff-side home hangs hundreds of feet above the sea. Many rustic and unrefined homes sit hidden from view on private dirt roads. Big Sur's homes are as varied and unconventional as their inhabitants.

The elegant Ventana Resort and Nepenthe Restaurant were designed by renowned architects Kipp Stewart and Rowan Maiden, respectively. The distinctive Coast Gallery is housed in a large water tank. Many of Big Sur's commercial establishments embody the talents of master builders and craftsmen.

Strict zoning and building regulations, inaccessible terrain and a limited water supply have minimized population growth. The few rentals which do exist are usually spoken for well in advance.

The area is protected from overdevelopment by a combination of state and local laws. This Big Sur Local Coastal Program prevents any building within sight of Highway 1, except in visitor serving community centers. The state legislature has resolved that Highway 1 through Big Sur shall forever remain a rural, two lane highway.

Big Sur's mild climate is profoundly affected by the insulating qualities of the Pacific Ocean, which cools the air in the summer months and warms it in the cooler times. The seasons are not as pronounced as other geographic sections of the American country. The mountain range geographically influences the winds and weather. No two successive days are the same here.

The rainy season, November through April is thought of as winter, although mild temperatures of 40 to 60 degrees predominate. Between rain storms, Big Sur gets some of its nicest, sunniest days. Rains may be weeks apart, yet the average annual rainfall along the coast often reaches 40 to 60 inches. The mountain's higher elevations receive 50 to 100 inches.

The dry season from May to October, rarely brings rain. Spring and fall often display the most pleasant weather. Nights and mornings at any time of the year suggest sweaters.

It is from scenic Highway 1 that most visitors contemplate the 80 mile length of Big Sur's rich resources. The two-lane road soars and zigzags along its precarious perches on the westernmost edges of the Santa Lucia Mountains as they stoop forward and continuously dive into the Pacific on California's central coast. Along the coastal road, from south of Carmel to near San Simeon, rising and falling land masses intervene between gently undulating pastures, brief encounters with redwood forests, and clefts and chasms often spanned by graceful arched bridges.
(Photo by Jim Neill)

A morning fog often characterizes the summer months of June, July and August. The soft sea fog blurs the contours of the coastline and hillsides. Grey water and grey haze combine offshore in a dim and misty world. The natural air conditioning usually burns off by noon, giving way to a warm, sunny day. Quite often, the Big Sur Valley, protected by a western ridge, remains clear when the coast is enshrouded in fog.

The fog forms when warm air heated by the sun mixes with the cool temperatures of the ocean waters. The sea breezes distribute the haze, adding mercurial dimension to the majestic countryside. Each setting takes on new contours as the haze moves in and out of canyons and lights a green meadow. The fog provides moisture and nourishment to the lush vegetation during the dry season.

Over the first set of ridges to the east, lies the inaccessible Big Sur back country, seldom seen by visitors. The weather here varies from the milder coastal climate. The summer heat is more intense and winter is more severe. The significant rainfall of the back country during the rainy season runs off through the two rivers and the creeks which flow westward to the ocean. Excessive rainfall in the back country has caused the disastrous flooding and mudslides to Big Sur's lower reaches in the past.

Henry Miller, the renowned author, wrote of the back county in his 1957 book *Big Sur and the Oranges of Hieronymus Bosch: Back of the ridge which overshadows us is a wilderness in which scarcely anyone ever sets foot. It is a great forest and game reserve, intended to be set apart forever. At night one feels the silence all about,*

a silence which begins far back of the ridge and which creeps in with the fog and the stars, with the warm valley winds, and which carries in its folds a mystery as deep as the earth's own. A magnetic, healing ambiance. Whoever settles here hopes that he will be the last invader. The very look of the land makes one long to keep it intact—the spiritual reserve of a few bright spirits.

Geology of the Region—The lands structural tendency is to the west. Thrust movements along the Sur fault and Sur Hill fault have played forceful roles in the geologic development of the steep and rugged coastal margin. The major rocks: the Sur series gneiss, the Franciscan, and Santa Margarita formations have been tilted at angles of 30 to 60 degrees to the northeast along the two faults.

More than 200 million years ago an immense stratum of sedimentary rocks amassed mostly below the sea, to form the Sur series gneiss. Later an invasion of molten rock crystallized far below the earth's surface as today's Santa Lucia granite.

Perhaps 100 million years later, sediments formed by erosion of mountain areas to the east and possibly lands to the west, were deposited in a sinking trough to form the sands, muds, and cherts of the Franciscan formation. Intermittent volcanic activity transpired, some of it below sea level.

About 20 million years ago, the seas advanced eastward several miles from today's coastline. About ten to fifteen million years ago the land mass was elevated and erosion created the sandy deposits of the Santa Margarita formation at the western rim.

Thrust faulting persisted and was followed later by a series of vertical uplifts. The main part of the mountain range raised 3,000 to 5,000 feet in a southwest direction. Westward tilting and uplifting continued until Recent time. Such forces have created the narrow valleys cut into the mountains by westward flowing streams, and marine terraces along the coast like those at Pacific Valley and the Pt. Sur Lighthouse Flats.

In More Detail

The Rocky Coast of Big Sur

Few approachable beaches exist because of the hazardous terrain and high cliffs. Some may be reached by climbing down the rocks, but this is often dangerous. Safe beaches are listed in the landmark section of this booklet. Rip tides and treacherous currents make swimming generally unsafe. No harbors exist along the remote coast for ninety miles from Monterey to San Simeon. Pfeiffer Cove, about thirty miles south of Carmel offers the only safe anchorage for small boats

Surf pounds the jagged cliffs and rocks that rise from the sea, slowly wearing away the rock, breaking it into smaller pieces, sculpting it into natural arches, ledges and sea caves. Artists and poets, geologists and philosophers have found inspiration on this rocky, surf beaten coast of Big Sur. Of special interest to botanists and zoologists is the underwater park totaling 6,361 acres located at Julia Pfeiffer-Burns State park on the southern coast, and the rocky coastline from the Carmel River to San Carpoforo Creek (on the extreme southern end of the Big Sur coast) that serves as a 9,421 acre refuge for the protected sea otter. The protrusive sea stacks seen along the coast just offshore are remnants of an earlier coastline.
(Photo by Larry French)

seeking refuge from the north wind.

The rocky shoreline functions as a natural habitat for multitudes of shellfish and marine life. The thick kelp beds, just offshore, serve as the protected sea otter's playground.

The sea stacks protruding from the water have broken off from the granite and basaltic rock cliffs over many years. An obvious display of these ancient formations jut from the water just offshore between Rocky and Bixby Creeks. In some locations, erosion from pounding waves has sculpted some stacks into natural arches.

The Santa Lucia Mountains

Big Sur is situated along the first set of mountain ridges which rise to more than 3,500 feet from the ocean. The Santa Lucia's are a double range, and in a few places, triple. The highest of the mountains, *Junipero Serra* rises to 5,862 feet.

The Spanish explorer Vizcaino named the range in 1602 as he sailed up the Pacific Coast. The range begins in the southern part of Carmel Valley in Monterey County. It extends for 120 miles southeast into San Luis Obispo County and ends near Point San Luis, north of the Santa Barbara Channel.

The northern section of the range stretches the entire length of the Big Sur coast. The mountains stretch eastward to the Salinas Valley, a distance of approximately 35 miles. On the inland side, the unique Santa Lucia fir grows. This beautiful symmetrical tree is found nowhere else in the world. Chaparral, a cover of shrubs, grasses and trees grows over the coastal range.

Hundreds of valuable minerals have been found, including gold and jade in quantity. In places, large deposits of granite and limestone occur, such as at Granite Peak and *Pico Blanco's* 500 acres of limestone. Mining claims exist in the mountains of the south coast. The U.S. Forest Service exercises control over the issuance of mining permits.

Hundreds of streams flow from the mountains to the Big and Little Sur Rivers, or flow directly into the ocean. A number of natural hot springs occur. Tassajara Hot Springs, open to the public by reservation only, can be reached by dialing the Monterey operator and asking for

"toll station 1." The hot springs at the Esalen Institute on the south coast are reserved for guests.

The Big Sur River drains forty six square miles of creeks from the mountains—some 30,000 acres. It flows down from the hills through the Pfeiffer-Big Sur State Park and crosses under the highway near the park's entrance. The channel widens and it turns and flows northward through the valley. Several campgrounds and resorts are located along its wooded banks. Five miles downstream, at the valley's northern end in the Andrew Molera State Park, it turns westward and flows into the ocean. In the summer, the river is mistaken for a creek, but during the rainy season it often overflows its banks.

The Little Sur River drains an area of the range's northern section. It runs through a portion of the private El Sur Ranch along the Old Coast Road and empties into the ocean some five miles north of the Big Sur River's mouth.

The Santa Lucia Mountains sing of a striking geologic history which originated over fifteen millions years ago when the mountains were covered by the sea. A profound elevation of the area occurred over time and at least part of the uplifting took place along the Sur fault zone.

The Big Sur River probably began as a westward flowing stream down the slope of the Santa Lucia Mountains. Confirmation of uplifting from less than a million years ago can

be observed in the terraces left along the present day course of the river.

About a million years ago, the river ran much higher. Benches and terraces left in its ancient path sit 300 feet above its current level. Vertical uplifting and westward tilting caused the river to cut deeper into its channel. The gravel terraces also indicate that the river at one time ran westward from the present gorge area in the Pfeiffer — Big Sur State Park along the Sur Hill and Sur fault zones. Present characteristics of the Big Sur Valley are a result of the Recent geologic forces mentioned above, along with the effects of erosion caused by running water.

*This aerial view of the northern coast of Big Sur allows one to visualize the seldom seen undeveloped **Ventana Wilderness** and back country to the east of Big Sur. Big Sur is 52 miles long and three to nine miles in width. The whole of Big Sur includes some 165,000 acres of which 68% is **Los Padres National Forest Land**; about 29% belongs to private citizens and 3% is in state ownership. Most people agree (or disagree) that the north-south boundaries of Big Sur are **Rocky Creek** (on the coastline near the center of this photograph) and the Monterey- San Luis Obispo County line almost 60 miles to the south. On the right side of the photo along the coastline, the **Old Coast Road** travels inland on the north side of **Bixby Bridge** and then turns southward over the mountains. On the extreme left side of the photograph **Palo Colorado Canyon** extends in a southeast diagonal direction.* (Photo Courtesy of Air Photo Co.)

The Santa Lucia Mountains of Big Sur abruptly ascend from the sea to lofty altitudes of over 3,000 feet within a range of three miles from the coastline. Beyond this first set of ridges the mountains rise to almost 6,000 feet. The botanical wealth of the range is as great as its mineral resources. The mountains are rich in endemic and disjunct plant species as well as being the northern and southern distributional limit of many more widely distributed species. The famous field botanists Thomas Coulter and David Douglas explored the Santa Lucia Mountains in the 1830's and found the unique Santa Lucia fir (Abies bracteata), *the rarest and most unusual fir in North America. It is found in no other place in the world than these mountains.*
(Photo by John Osterman)

The Los Padres National Forest and Ventana Wilderness

The U.S. Forest Service owns most of the land in the Monterey County section of the Santa Lucia Mountains. The northern section of the Los Padres National Forest parallels the Big Sur coast and covers some 340,000 acres. Within the national forest lies 159,000 acres of Ventana Wilderness.

Although the forest and wilderness areas are one in the same, each has certain restrictions. The Wilderness Act of 1964 states that no mechanized equipment is allowed within the wilderness area. Man made improvements are disallowed. Hunting is prohibited and thus creates an unofficial wildlife sanctuary.

The national forest land is used for various purposes by the public. The forest service issues permits for grazing, botanical research, mining and logging.

A well designed system of trails leads experienced hikers over the ridges and into the canyons of the rugged Ventana Wilderness. Forest rangers patrol the hiking area on horseback and carry radios for emergency communication. Camping areas have been set aside along the trails. A permit must be obtained at the originating ranger station for campfires in designated areas. Persons planning to hike into the Ventana Wilderness can obtain information from the ranger stations listed below or from the Monterey District Ranger's Office, U.S. Forest Service District Headquarters, 406 South Mildred Street, King City, CA 93930. Information, maps and permits can be obtained from the following forest service stations:

Trails leading from the northern section - Bottcher's Gap Station, eight miles up Palo Colorado Canyon.

Trails leading from the Big Sur Valley Area - Big Sur Station, located beside the highway maintenance station in the valley.

Trails leading from Pacific Valley - Pacific Valley Station, 33 miles south of Big Sur Valley.

Trails leading from the southern section - Salmon Creek Station, 45 miles south of the Big Sur Valley.

Wildlife of the Ventana Wilderness—The country's largest population of mountain lions *(Felis concolor)* inhabit the Santa Lucia Mountains. One lion is stocked for each ten square miles of wilderness area. Wild pigs were introduced in the 1920's. Many Big Sur residents have seen mountain lions and wild pigs on the highway at night.

Some rivers and streams support fresh water fish species such as native rainbow trout and the introduced German brown trout. Steelhead migrate up the Big and Little Sur rivers and those streams which empty directly into the ocean.

Occasionally, the endangered southern bald eagle is spotted. The extremely rare and endangered American Peregrine falcon lives in the southern section.

The fabulous Bixby Bridge on the northern coast of Big Sur is one of the most photographed bridges in the west. Before it was constructed over the steep gorge where Bixby Creek runs into the ocean, early travelers got to Big Sur by way of the Old Coast Road that turns inland on the north side of the bridge. The bridge is notable because of the 320 foot length of the central span and the height of 260 feet above the creek. It is hollow inside and the small doors on the long columns allow workmen to go inside and inspect for cracks. (Photo by Thomas Gundelfinger)

Landmarks, Businesses
& Points of Interest
Along the Big Sur Coast

Along the sheer edge of western America, the landmarks of Big Sur weave a natural tour de force. For eighty miles, the Santa Lucia Mountains stoop forward and dive into the Pacific Ocean.

Man's own stunning creation, Coast Highway One, snakes along mountain ledges for the length of Big Sur. Flanked on the west by the sea, it is from this two-lane road that most people contemplate the rich resources of Sur Country.

Four California state parks offer easy walks, and sometimes, camping, picnicking, and beach access. Select Los Padres National Forest areas provide similar services. Serious hikers can confront the great Ventana Wilderness. On the remaining property, private landowners enforce trespassing laws.

Long ago, geological forces sculpted and splintered the land into three regions: the *North Coast*, *Big Sur Valley*, and *South Coast*. Dawning some ten miles south of Carmel, the *North Coast* originates near Rocky Creek. Gently undulating pastures intervene between jagged cliffs, lofty headlands, clefts, and chasms for twelve miles to the threshold of the valley.

A ridge separates the *Big Sur Valley* from the coastline for over five miles. Along its eastern feet, the Big Sur River channels northward. The road, often girded by tall redwoods, wanders one to two miles inland past a succession of rustic and elegant inns, campgrounds, shops, the library, and post office.

Beyond this, the less populated and wilder *South Coast* dramatically soars and zigzags for sixty miles. Finally, just past Monterey County, the rising and falling land masses subside to near sea level.

The following pages portray the rapture of its present and past. For the sake of orientation, this excursion exceeds Big Sur's borders. It begins on Highway One, eight miles south of Carmel and ends at the Hearst Castle in San Simeon.

Full-page maps correspond to its regions. Approximate distances from the Pfeiffer Big Sur State Park, (0), follow each listing. "N," and "S," symbolize a north or south perspective to the park, in the heart of the valley. "E," or "W," marks a mountainside or seaward position.

The North Coast

MALPASO CREEK (21.0 N) These steep canyon walls proposed a challenge to early travelers, inspiring Spaniards to label it as a "bad pass." Later, it provided early ranchers with an excellent place for breaking horses.

Once over the bridge, just past Carmel Highlands, and eight miles south of Carmel, a panorama of land and seascapes fire the imagination. Monterey cypress trees dot eastern hillsides and line the oceanside of Highway One, concealing the private Otter Cove area.

GARRAPATA STATE PARK (20.5 N) For the next four miles, numerous trails lead from almost every highway turnout to ocean bluffs and some venture into eastern canyons and ridges. Most approaches are marked only by small numbered signs. Stay on the trails within the park, as trespassing laws are strictly enforced by adjacent landowners. Please respect their rights.

The only safe waterfront access is at the highly visible Garrapata Beach at the 3,067 acre preserve's southern border. Enjoy the views from the sage and ice plant lined paths leading to the west, but don't approach its craggy margin. The surf is subject to life threatening waves and currents, which create hazardous conditions for rock climbing, swimming, and wading.

SOBERANES POINT (19.2 NW) is marked by an eastern stand of cypress trees at the highway, perhaps planted as a wind break by the homesteaders for whom it is named. From a distance, this sculptural promontory can best be identified by its feminine contours.

Take the trail around the headland for one of the coast's better opportunities to intimately consider the mercurial ocean, the jumble of bluffs, and coves, and distant views of the land and seascapes. On the eastern side of the highway, near the Soberanes Barn, the 1.5 mile Soberanes Canyon and three mile rocky Ridge Trails ascend the hills for a rare offering of the diverse ecosystems of the northern Santa Lucia Mountains.

This photograph taken in 1932 shows the new highway bridge in the foreground and the old road bridge that actually passed over the beach. The old road can be seen to the left of the new bridge as it switched back over the mountains. The old bridge has since been destroyed. The present day Garrapata Creek bridge has a central span of 150 feet and a height of 95 feet above the creek. The Garrapata Beach nearby is a popular spot for visitors.
(Lewis Josselyn Photo from the Pat Hathaway Collection)

GRANITE CANYON (18.3 N) North of the bridge, a fence surrounds the Marine Toxicology Studies Laboratory of the California Department of Fish and Game that is closed to the public. Submarine scientists evaluate the effects of pollutants, such as petroleum and hydrocarbons, on marine life and set acceptable standards for maintaining a healthy marine ecosystem. Collaborating with other groups, their research identifies toxic hot spots in California's bays and estuaries.

From here, the long, white strand of Garrapata Beach captures your attention. Look in the far distance for a choice glimpse of a miniature version of Point Sur Rock with its 19th century lighthouse facility atop. Every 15 seconds, the powerful light beams a signal that is seen for 23 miles.

GARRAPATA STATE BEACH (16.3 NW) From the turnout, its main entrance crosses a meadow of ice plant. Follow the well-marked pathway to the pristine beach.

Swimming and wading are highly discouraged due to the hazardous undertow and unpredictable wave patterns. Like other state park trails, it opens and closes with the sun. Dogs should be on leashes.

GARRAPATA CREEK (16.5 N) marks the southernmost border of the park. Pronounced *gerh-ah-PAH-tah*, and Spanish for "tick," the epitaph probably evolved from early settlers, who contended with a glut of these insects in the canyon.

ROCKY POINT RESTAURANT (15.2 NW) Lunch, dinner, and cocktails are served just a hundred feet above the rocky shoreline. Sweeping views of the coastline include Rocky Creek Bridge, breaching whales, and pastel sunsets. Renowned for its generous portions and steak and seafood, dinner reservations are essential. (408) 624-2933.

Down the hill from Rocky Point at the shoreline, wave action has carved a natural arch from a cliff. Further on, Rocky Creek Bridge is the first of Big Sur's graceful spans to enthrall the visual sense. It is often mistaken for its larger sibling, Bixby Bridge, in the next canyon. This area generally represents the actual threshold to Big Sur.

PALO COLORADO CANYON (15.3 NE) Over millions of years, vertical motion along the Palo Colorado Fault has aided in the creation of the spectacular topography of the tip-tilted land of Big Sur. In more recent times, the Spanish of the early 19th century named the canyon for its plentiful stands of ancient redwoods, *Sequoia sempervirens*.

Girded by these tall trees, abundant flora, small cabins, and a creek, the one and a half lane winding road can only be driven cautiously by the familiar or by hikers going to Bottcher's Gap. Four miles in, the road widens and a sunny, arid climate prevails.

BOTTCHER'S GAP, further in and eight miles east of Highway One, at 2100 feet, hosts a U.S. Forest Service tent campground amid oaks and madrone. The three to eight mile long Skinner Ridge Trails begin here and offer views of the ocean, Little Sur River Gorge, Ventana Cone, Double Cone, and South Ventana Cone; and "The Window," a horseshoe shaped gap between two mountains which creates a natural frame for wilderness scenes. See Ventana Wilderness hiking information on page 10.

NOTLEY'S LANDING (15.2 NW) From 1898 to 1907, a small village and lumber enterprise occupied the meadow south and oceanside of Palo Colorado. After harvesting in nearby canyons, tanbark oak, valuable for its tannic acid; and other timbers were transported by mules, milled and processed, and finally sent down a long

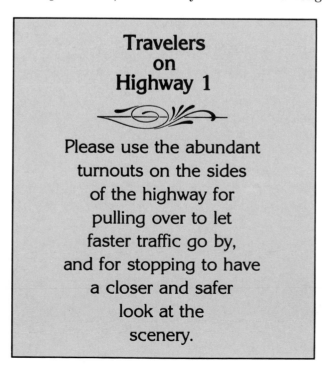

Travelers
on
Highway 1

Please use the abundant
turnouts on the sides
of the highway for
pulling over to let
faster traffic go by,
and for stopping to have
a closer and safer
look at the
scenery.

13

chute to vessels at the makeshift landing.

More often than not, gaiety and accordion music resounded from Godfrey Notley's cliffside dance hall, attracting folks from miles around. Legends of the rip roarious era were so powerful that the Carmel poet Robinson Jeffers immortalized it in his narrative poem *Mara*.

Around the turn of the 19th century, the lumber or lime industries at various coastal landings boosted the population to today's level of about 1500. It dwindled when these resources were depleted. The abandoned landings gained notoriety during Prohibition when they were rumored to have been used for smuggling liquor.

ROCKY CREEK BRIDGE (13.7 N) A concrete arch of 239 feet carries the straight section of road 150 feet above the mouth of Rocky Creek. The early Spanish called it *rio piedras*, perhaps inspired by an abundance of rocks.

LONG RIDGE separates Rocky and Bixby Canyons. Just offshore from the winding approach, tides rip over sea stacks: time-worn boulders that have broken away from the granite and basalt cliffs.

OLD COAST ROAD (13.2 NE) Traveling eastward at Bixby Bridge's north side, the unpaved road treks inland for 14 miles over Santa Lucia' slopes and ends near the mouth of the Big Sur Valley. Prior to Bixby Bridge and the highway's completion in the 1930s, a sojourn along this passage was a necessity. Still somewhat of a challenge, it carries certain responsibilities: proceed slowly with caution and observe a serious respect for the private land, always just inches off the drive.

On its northern end, you briefly parallel the south fork of the Little Sur River. On the southern descent, pull off at a turnout and witness the world below like one of the red-tail hawks soaring on the wind currents of a nearby canyon: To the north, Point Sur resembles a fairy tale island and the tiny ribbon of highway far below fits the same fable. To the south, the Big Sur River forms a boomerang at the valley's northern end in Andrew Molera State Park as it cuts westward to unite with the sea.

BIXBY BRIDGE (13.2 N) towers 260 feet above the creek and is supported by a graceful, 320 foot arch that links the steep walls of Bixby Canyon. Most people agree that this concrete sculpture is the most stunning of Big Sur's many bridges.

On completion in 1932, "Rainbow bridge," as it was often called, was proclaimed as an

The Big Sur River flows northward through the Andrew Molera State Park to its mouth only a short distance to the west. Highway 1, seen here to the left of the photograph entering the Big Sur Valley, runs parallel to the river. With the opening of the walk-in campground at Andrew Molera State Park in 1972, the public now has access to the beach south of the river's mouth that eventually connects with Pfeiffer Beach some three miles further on. Pfeiffer Ridge is in the back-ground.
(Photo by Linda Lloyd)

On November 23, 1932 when this photograph was taken, the Bixby Creek Bridge was dedicated and opened for use by the public. Notice the old cars of the time in the background. At the time of construction it was known as Rainbow Bridge after the bow-shape of the arch-span. (Lewis Josselyn Photo from the Pat Hathaway Collection)

engineering marvel. Today, its $250,000 construction cost wouldn't even purchase a small cabin in these hills. Six hundred thousand pounds of reinforcing steel support the arch, along with 6,600 cubic yards of concrete, the equivalent of 825 concrete truck loads today.

At the highway turnout on the bridge's northwest side, Mrs. Lyndon Johnson dedicated this spectacular drive as California's first scenic highway in a September, 1966 ceremony. The Sharpe Restaurant existed here until some time after 1932 and the Gallatin family of Monterey later operated the Crocodile's Tail Restaurant, which would be disallowed with today's coastal plan.

The concrete foundation remains of Bixby Landing stand nearby, remindful of the lime smelting operation and canyon community which thrived on its lime and lumber resources from 1907 to 1910. Japanese and Italian workers filled the forest, cutting firewood, and operating the kilns. Lime-filled barrels were transported along a cabled tramway up the ridge and three miles over the canyon. At Bixby Landing, they were rolled down a chute to market-bound boats.

Charlie Bixby, a popular figure in the early Big Sur community, supervised and built most of the wagon roads from Carmel Highlands to his own canyon. Before Bixby's arrival, the stream was called Mill Creek after a saw mill operation nearby.

HURRICANE POINT (11.9 NW) The north coast's loftiest and most airy headland, is marked by a steep highway approach, prevailing westerly winds, and boulders that border the seaward

The beach and lagoon in the foreground mark the spot where the Little Sur River runs into the ocean. The beach at the little river's mouth is private but the view from the highway above is free for the taking. Highway 1 winds its way north along the edge of the mountains to the 800 foot Hurricane Point, a Big Sur landmark characterized by strong, gusty winds and huge boulders that encircle the highway turnout. The plateau at the bottom of the promontory is littered with irretrievable vehicles whose drivers took the sharp curve with too much speed and too little attention.
(Photo by John Osterman)

side of the turnout. From the 800 foot overhang, you can ponder the infinitely beautiful Point Sur Rock to the south and the graceful symmetry of Bixby Bridge to the north. Directly below, an ancient marine terrace is littered with the remains of irretrievable vehicles—reminders that the next few miles south, the Sierra Hill section from this point to Little Sur River commands a driver's full attention or a willingness to pull off at a turnout for a closer look around.

LITTLE SUR RIVER (9.6 N) A horsehoe-shaped highway descent leads into the mouth of the Little Sur Valley where its river aims seaward after draining a northern section of Santa Lucia's creeks. The Spaniards of the late 1700s called it *rio chiquito del Sur,* "The little river to the south," but early residents knew it simply as "Little River."

Just west of the low-lying highway bridge, the river forms a lagoon behind a sandbar that prevents its ocean reach in the dry season. But during winter and spring rains, it flows into the ocean, often creating aquamarine waters offshore from its heavy lime deposits.

In the distant river valley, 3,709 foot *Pico Blanco* interrupts the sky with its lime-splattered

peak that has been a navigational aid to mariners for centuries. The native Esselen Indians revered it as "the sacred birthplace of both man and beast." Today, ownership is shared by the U.S. Forest Service and a private mining company.

Years ago, an old miner of Pico Blanco and homesteader of nearby land, told a story of digging into an opening which eventually revealed a cave system inside, complete with stalactites, stalagmites, albino fish and glowing insects. While no evidence of this has been located, underground streams could have carved such a system from the porous limestone.

Around the turn of the 19th century, a resort flourished in an area about a mile up river from the highway bridge. Idlewild, popular among fishermen and nature lovers, took its name from "The *Idylwild,*" a popular poem of the time that portrayed country life.

The Little Sur River beach and surrounding land are privately owned and the trespassing warnings are strictly enforced. Like most Big Sur beaches, severe undertow and unforeseeable waves here make swimming and even wading hazardous.

POINT SUR (7.5 NW) From a distance, the 350 foot volcanic rock emerges like an island, but it is actually linked to land by a sandbar. This prominent chunk of resistant pillow lava is derived from a geologic process which occurred some 100 million years ago.

Point Sur is now a state historic landmark, offering weekly walking tours of the 19th century lighthouse facility, its museum and gift shop. Equally appealing is the unhurried opportunity to enjoy its diverse views. Volunteers from the Big Sur Natural History Association are usually present, as well as someone from the Cetacean Society during the winter migration of the California grey whales. Even on warm days, visitors should dress for cool, windy weather. Phone for tour information. (408) 625-4419.

Atop the uninhabited rock, historic buildings include the stone tower lighthouse on the northwest corner. Today it is unmanned and operates on an automated system administered by the Coast Guard in Monterey. Mariners at sea are assisted by radio signals, a fog horn trumpeting tones audible for ten miles during poor visibility, and a powerful light that is distinct for 23 miles seaward.

Local ranchers accessed the rock along 395 wooden steps up its eastern side to construct the lighthouse in 1899 and supplies were hoisted up by pack animals pulling a tramway. Kerosene oil powered the first light and a pendulum rotated the lens.

Prior to this, suspenseful shipwrecks occurred. In 1872, the S. S. Los Angeles met its demise near Point Sur, killing most of the people aboard. When the steamship Venture foundered and sank near the Little Sur River mouth in 1879, local ranchers managed to salvage some of its cargo, furnishing their rustic cabins with fine linens and tooling over the Big Sur Hills in the knock-down wagons for years afterwards. The navy's airship Macon crash landed in the ocean south of Point Sur in February 1935 after a strong gust of wind crumbled a section of the dirigible. A quick rescue saved 78 of the 81 men aboard.

The Little Sur River flows under the low-lying highway bridge and flows into the ocean only a short distance away. The meadow on the east side of the bridge was the site of a road camp that housed the convict labor sent down from San Quentin and other prisons around the state for the construction of Highway 1 in 1928. In the right foreground stand the windswept cypress trees that are endemic to Monterey County. (Photo by John Osterman)

THE FORMER POINT SUR NAVAL FACILITY (7.3 NW) sits at the base of the big rock and is off-limits to the public. Until the late 1980s, a small crew conducted oceanographic research here. While its future is uncertain, the property will probably be retained by the navy for environmental research. Trespassing laws are strictly enforced on the private ranch land and beach below the rock. **Lighthouse Flats,** a level stretch of roadway, runs south for two miles from Point Sur to the Big Sur Valley's entrance.

OLD COAST ROAD (4.5 NE) The southern entrance—exit to the unpaved county road sits opposite the Andrew Molera State Park entrance. It traverses the mountains for 14 winding miles, and terminates on the northern side of Bixby Bridge. Drive it only with extreme caution and a serious respect for the unapproachable private property on either side. See page 14 for more information.

ANDREW MOLERA STATE PARK (4.5 NW) begins at the Big Sur Valley's northern threshold and offers walk-in camping and day use of its beach and trail system. Cars are left in the parking area near the fee and information station.

Within Molera's 4,785 acre borders, Pfeiffer Ridge slices through the southwest portion, dropping to some four miles of cliffside ocean frontage, including a mile of prime beach; and falls on the east to the Big Sur River which channels some two miles northward within the preserve, cuts west, and flows into the ocean between a sandbar and small promontory. The land sweeps lushly northward over meadows and flatland. Much of the park lies within its eastern section that climbs into the hills, south of the Old Coast Road entrance.

Hiking trails lead into these eastern hills from the Molera Barn under a highway tunnel. To the west, the beach is less than a mile away along flat terrain, dotted with native herbs, grasses, and wildflowers. Looking at the eastern mountains from this point, Pico Blanco with its white, limestone peak dominates the skyline.

At the river mouth and beach, many species of ducks, terns, and shorebirds flourish within the bird sanctuary. Just offshore, a rocky reef extends to the south. To the northwest, and south of Point Sur, a detached submerged reef, Sur Breakers, averts large swells from the river mouth area.

In this aerial view of the northern outskirts of the Big Sur Valley and the Valley itself, the Little Sur River flows under the low-lying bridge where the highway follows a horseshoe-shaped path on the left side of the photo. The river forms a lagoon on the private beach where it unites with the Pacific Ocean. The huge mountain directly above the river is Pico Blanco, once said by the coastal Indians to be the "sacred birthplace of man and beast." Point Sur sits shoreward of a sandbar at the right of the photo; the tiny cluster of buildings at the foot of the "Big Rock" of Point Sur is the Point Sur Naval Facility. The two points to the south are Cooper and Pfeiffer points directly beside one another. To the east of these points Pfeiffer Ridge separates the Big Sur Valley from the coastline. Post Summit and Mount Manuel respectively stand to the east of the valley. The steep and rugged topography of the area is suggestive of a complex geologic history.
(Photo Courtesy of Air Photo Co.)

This land was once part of the great Rancho El Sur, a 9,000 acre Spanish land grant, deeded shortly after 1834 to Juan Bautista Cooper, a Yankee trader and sea captain. Big Sur's grammar school and Cooper Point, the next promontory to the south, are named for him. See page 42.

The park represents what was once the southern section of Rancho El Sur, which later belonged to Cooper's grandson, Andrew Molera, who was best known for his imposing stature and generosity, and the buffalo he brought here and tried unsuccessfully to cross-breed with cattle. In the northwest section, only the old foundation and machines remain from Molera's creamery, where he produced Monterey Jack cheese, selling it in Monterey markets for six cents a pound. However, other time worn Molera

Rancheria buildings from this era still stand in Creamery Meadow. Big Sur's oldest structure, the Cooper Cabin, is located beyond the trail camp in a eucalyptus grove.

In 1965, Frances Molera donated a portion of this land to the Nature Conservancy in honor of her brother. Through their efforts, it was deeded to the state and opened as a park in 1972, and has since been enlarged by additional land purchases.

MOLERA TRAIL RIDES (408) 625-8664, a private concession located in a barn near the parking area, operates seasonally and features two hour guided tours on horseback that negotiate 6 miles of diverse trails within the preserve.

The 350 foot rock of Point Sur sits offshore of a sandbar that gives the rock the pretense of being an island. The signal tower of the lighthouse sits on a promontory on the northwest end of the rock at 270 feet above the sea. The buildings atop Point Sur are uninhabited at present and the lighthouse operation is run by computer. The powerful light can be seen for 23 miles at sea and the compressed air fog diaphone can be heard for 10 miles. Underwater sound detectors locate the beat of the ship's propellors. There are virtually no shipwrecks on the coast today due to modern technology, but when the light was constructed in 1899 by local ranchers, this area of the California coast was known as the graveyard of the Pacific. Only a few years ago portions of the 19th century ships which wrecked near the light were visible at low tide. Point Sur and the beach below are private. (Photos by: John Osterman)

Highway One enters the northern end of the Big Sur Valley. Traveling one to two miles inland, the flat section of road is skirted on the east by the Santa Lucia Mountains and to the west by its river and a ridge separating it from the ocean. Much of the population exists along its six mile succession of rustic inns, campgrounds, and businesses.
(Photo by Heidi McGurrin)

Big Sur Valley

Commercial listings are complimentary. For more information, phone or write to their specific geographic locations on Highway One. Or send a self-addressed, stamped envelope to request information from the Big Sur Chamber of Commerce, P.O. Box 87, Big Sur, CA 93920; (408) 667-2100.

RIVER INN RESORT (2.0 NW) is nestled alongside the River with a sprawling lawn. Services include a BP gas station, motel, grocery store with delicatessen and pizza, patio espresso and dessert bar; and breakfast, lunch, dinner, and cocktails served outside or in the rustic, redwood beamed dining room. Weekends are highlighted by live entertainment. Poetry readings are held on Tuesday evenings. Riverside, you'll find a large deck, motel suites; and a heated swimming pool for guests, residents by membership, and day use by visitors for a fee. (408) 667-2700; (800) 548-3610; (408) 625-5255.

HEARTBEAT GIFT SHOP, beside River Inn's restaurant, specializes in musical instruments and unusual gift and personal items. 667-2557.

THE VILLAGE SHOPS (2.1 NW) are located just south of River Inn's grocery store. Shops include an art gallery, Monique's Original Clothing Designs, an English pub, hand woven designs by a local artisan, and BIG SUR GARAGE AND TOWING, (408) 667-2181, which opens daily, providing full service and repairs, and 24 hour emergency road assistance.

BIG SUR CAMPGROUND AND CABINS (1.7 NW) The Big Sur River meanders past the redwood filled enclave with its 82 tent and RV sites, laundry, bath houses, small store, playground with basketball/volleyball court, and swimming in the river. Reservations are recommended from May to September and year round for the 12 cabins, some with kitchens and fireplaces. (408) 667-2322.

BIG SUR HEALTH CENTER (1.8 NW) is accessed by the Big Sur Campground entrance. With the closest medical facility being 30 miles to the north, this invaluable, nonprofit organization provides health care to residents by appointment, and to visitors only for medical emergencies. Open Mondays, Wednesdays, Fridays, and on Tuesdays for psychological and nutritional counseling. Donations are essential and appreciated. (408) 667-2580.

SANTA LUCIA MISSION (1.7 NW) of the All Saint's Episcopal Church in Carmel is located beside the health center. Outdoor services are held beside the river on Sundays at 11 A.M. in the summer and the first Sunday of each winter month. (408) 624-3883.

RIVERSIDE CAMPGROUND AND CABINS (1.6 NW) has 45 campsites, comfortable cabins, and overnight rooms beside the river or among the redwoods with laundry and playground facilities. (408) 667-2414.

BIG SUR LIBRARY (1.2 NE) is open to residents and visitors on Mondays and Fridays from 1:00 to 5:00 P.M., Wednesdays 10:00 A.M. to 5:00 P.M., and Saturdays from Noon to 5:00 P.M. 667-2537.

RIPPLEWOOD RESORT (1.2 NE) is family operated and features a Chevron gas station, general store, cabins, and cafe. Visitors and locals alike return again and again for more of the home style breakfasts, lunches, and Mexican dinners. Nine cozy cabins, some with fireplaces and kitchens, are tucked beneath the redwoods beside the rippling Big Sur River. Another six units border peaceful tree-lined meadows. Visit the Big Sur Library located on the premises. Reservations for Ripplewood: (408) 667-2242.

GLEN OAKS MOTEL (1.3 NE) Owned by one of Big Sur's most respected long time residents, these clean and comfortable 15 units and a cottage are set amidst native trees and colorful gardens. Credit cards are not accepted. 667-2105.

GLEN OAKS RESTAURANT (1.3 NW) Chefs Marilee and Forest Childs serve gourmet dinners nightly from 6:00 - 9:45 in a romantic setting, flattered by Marilee's original watercolor paintings. Reservations are made at 667-2623.

PANNY'S HAIR CARE (1.3 NW) Hair styling for men and women. Open Wednesday through Saturday by appointment. (408) 667-2101.

SAINT FRANCIS OF THE REDWOODS CATHOLIC CHAPEL (1.0 NW) As a part of the Carmel Mission Parish, mass is held every Sunday morning at 10:30. (408) 624-1271.

FERNWOOD RESORT (0.7 NW) includes a Union 76 gas station, grocery store, video rental shop, 12 motel units, a cocktail lounge and restaurant that serves American style food from 11:30 A.M. to 10:00 P.M. Set mostly among the redwoods, the 60 site campground offers some riverside hookups. (408) 667-2422.

BIG SUR LODGE (0 E) is located just inside the entrance to Pfeiffer Big Sur State Park and houses the motel office, a gift shop, grocery store and restaurant serving breakfast, lunch and dinner overlooking the Big Sur River. The 61 guest accommodations and swimming pool sit on a hill surrounded by mountains. All state park facilities are available to guests. Reservations P.O. Box 190, BS 93920. (408) 667-2171.

PFEIFFER BIG SUR STATE PARK (0 E) At the entrance kiosk, DPR personnel collect fees and offer information about day use, over 200 trailer and tent sites, and the private concession lodge within the park. Reservations for campsites are advisable from May through October and are made by calling Mistix at (800) 444-7275.

The gentle Big Sur River meanders westward through the diverse sanctuary on its way to the sea, draining 46 square miles of mountain streams. Many campsites, picnic areas and trails are located alongside its banks.

A nature trail system for hikers and miles of level roadway, weave throughout the forest, often arbored by redwoods and bays. Wildlife abound and even in daylight hours, black-tailed deer roam the woods. Raccoons are plentiful after nightfall and the little bandits often steal food in locked containers from campers.

The Pfeiffer name, pronounced Pie-fur, originates with one of the premier families who settled here. In 1944, the park was named for John Pfeiffer, who donated a portion of the 680 acres acquired by the state park commission in 1934. Currently, 861 acres extend from the entrance to Big Sur Station and eastward into the mountains (408) 667-2315.

BIG SUR RIVER BRIDGE (0.2 S) South of the park's approach, the River crosses under the highway. It arcs northward, flowing some five miles past campgrounds and resorts to the valley's end, cuts west and meets the ocean.

BIG SUR STATION—Multiagency Facility, (MAF) (0.7 SE) This sprawling enclave houses Administrative offices for the Big Sur District of DPR, California Department of Parks and Recreation, (408) 667-2315; Big Sur District Offices for (USFS), the U.S. Forest Service, (408) 667-2423; and the California Department of Transportation (Caltrans), (408) 667-2173.

In the administration buildings lobby, USFS and DPR personnel provide information to the public. The Sanders Conference Room memorializes Tom Sanders, a beloved resident and former chief of Caltrans in Big Sur until 1991, when he was tragically struck down near the Little Sur River Bridge. The room is also procurable to non-agency users for a fee.

At the Work Center, Caltrans and USFS occupy separate spaces for equipment and operations. The highly respected staff of Caltrans maintain Big Sur's only highway, often risking their lives during winter storms to keep it clear of mud and rock slides. In addition to sustaining and patrolling the forest, USFS is fully operational for combating fires, and the nearby helicopter pad assists with fire fighting and forest rescues.

Hiking trails lead from this, and other Monterey District forest service outposts listed on page 10. Information, maps, and permits for campfires in designated areas are obtained from the USFS in the lobby of the administration building. Some 75 paved parking spaces for hikers are located near the Pine Ridge trail head here. Within the Monterey District, the USFS operaters 11 drive-in campgrounds, some on the coast.

The 350,000 acre northern section of LOS PADRES NATIONAL FOREST sweeps eastward from the Big Sur coastline. Of this same land, 164,500 acres are classified as VENTANA WILDERNESS, an official wildlife sanctuary. Numerous campsites in the back country sit alongside trails that lead capable hikers over ridges, creeks, and through verdant canyons with rare views of the back country and ocean; and opportunities for intimacy with the diverse ecosystems of the Santa Lucia Mountains.

Pfeiffer Creek flows down Sycamore Canyon to unite with the ocean lagoon here at Pfeiffer Beach, one of the most beautiful of the Big Sur beaches. The dramatic land and rock seascape is characterized by tall sea cliffs with wave carved archs, offshore sea stacks, wind swept sand dunes, and a variety of shorebirds. Although its beauty is overwhelming, the gusty winds at Pfeiffer Beach often prove to be too much for the tenderfoot, and swimming is hazardous due to the strong currents. Michael and Barbara Pfeiffer, two of the earliest residents, homesteaded land nearby in 1869. (Photo by Linda Lloyd)

SYCAMORE CANYON ROAD (1.3 SW) descends into the canyon north of Pfeiffer Bridge and is the second turn west and south of Big Sur Station. The narrow road winds west two miles to Pfeiffer Beach's parking area. Travel it with caution, stay to the right, and yield to oncoming traffic where the road narrows to a single lane.

Recreational vehicles and anything larger than a mid-size car should definitely refrain from attempting this rugged, one and a half lane strip. Please do not approach or inconvenience the private homes and diverging roadways.

PFEIFFER BEACH, part of the Los Padres National Forest, opens at sunrise, and closes at sunset. Camping and fires are not allowed. With its abundant butterflies, archeological sites, and rare species of flora and fauna, this entire area deserves sensitive treatment. To help insure its ecological health, take nothing and leave nothing.

From the parking area, walk the path under a canopy of cypress trees alongside Pfeiffer Creek to the beach.

BIG SUR POST OFFICE - (1.7 SW) Open Monday to Friday, window hours are 8:30 A.M. to 5:00 P.M. Outgoing mail departs for town around 4:00 P.M. On Saturdays, it's best to drop your mail in the outside box for a 2:00 P.M. departure to town. Prior to its location here in 1987, residents were able to receive mail addressed simply to Big Sur, 93920, but today, a complete address must accompany correspondence. (408) 667-2305.

BIG SUR CENTER DELI AND GROCERY (1.7 SE) Located beside the post office, this complete grocery features a full service delicatessen and serves take-out pizzas after 5:00 P.M. 667-2225.

BIG SUR BAZAAR (1.7 SE) adjoins the Center Deli and features quality gift items, jewelry, pottery, clothing, music, video rentals, crafts, and local art. (408) 667-2197.

LOMA VISTA SHELL STATION AND GARDENS (1.8 S) sit atop a hill along the paved drive beside the Bazaar and is the last chance for gasoline for 23 miles to the south. Cacti, begonias in season, and firewood are sold. (408) 667-2818.

24

POST SUMMIT (2.3 SE) eclipses the steep grade of Post Hill which climbs for almost two miles from near Pfeiffer Big Sur State Park. Like the Pfeiffers, the Post name is forged into the annals of Big Sur's history. The Post homestead, now owned by Ventana as a private residence, still stands near the resort's entrance. See the historical photograph and caption on page 43.

VENTANA CAMPGROUND (2.4 SE) Sixty-two secluded tent sites are nestled in a redwood canyon along post Creek, with bathhouses and a nightly security patrol. RVs are not recommended. (408) 667-2688.

VENTANA RESORT (2.4 SE) continues to accumulate awards for everything from "one of the world's ten best country inns," to four stars in travel guides for its cuisine. Facing the sea on hillsides, the California modern structures of natural wood with tall ceilings and large, exposed beams were designed by renowned architect and Big Sur resident Kipp Stewart.

The cozy, 60 room inn is spread about the meadows on wooded slopes, amid a kaleidoscope of gardens. In addition to the two secluded swimming pools and two Japanese hot baths, many rooms have private hot tubs on a deck overlooking the forest, canyon, or ocean. Advance reservations should be made. 667-2331, 624-4812, 628-6500.

VENTANA RESTAURANT (2.4 SE) features continental cuisine and serves lunch, dinner, cocktails, and wines from an award winning list in an elegant three tiered room with view windows. Outside, the dining patio overhangs the world. Phone for dinner reservations.

THE STORE AT VENTANA (2.4 SE) beside the Ventana Restaurant, offers a selection of beautiful wares from far and near, including local specialties and works of fine art, in an intimate atmosphere of rustic elegance. Open daily, 9 A.M. to 10 P.M. (408) 667-2787.

BIG SUR FIRE BRIGADE (2.4 SW) Located on the west side of Highway One on property donated by the Post Ranch Inn, the firehouse was constructed in 1992 with publicity donated funds. Volunteers are responsible for structure fires from a northern point at the Little Sur River to the southern Monterey County Line. This invaluable, nonprofit organization depends on donations and receives no other funding. P.O. Box 520, Big Sur, CA 93920. (408) 667-2113.

Looking down on the Big Sur Valley to the south one can see why sunny days usually prevail as a result of the natural protection that the mountains to the east provide and the natural barrier that Pfeiffer Ridge provides from the ocean's wind and fog on the west. Highway 1 winds over the valley floor of the tiny village where tall redwoods stand ancient and aloof along the shoulders of the road and on the banks of the river. The soft sounds of chirping birds, a lazy little river, clean, fragrant air, and warm sunshine are all typical of "just another day" in the magical little valley of Big Sur.
(Photo by Ralph Fairfield)

POST RANCH INN (2.4 SW) Girded by the sea and mountains, the 30 room inn and glass-walled Sierra Mar restaurant sit on a cliffside ridge at 1100 feet, on the western portion of the former Post Ranch. Big Sur architect Mickey Muenning conceived the myriad styles of guest houses, focusing on privacy and the structures' conformance to the original landscape. A complete spa facility is open to guests. Reservations: (800) 527-2200, (408) 667-2200. P.O. Box 219, Big Sur, CA 93920.

POST RANCH MERCANTILE provides a catalog of signed goods from the Post Ranch Inn. To receive a copy write P.O. Box 245, Big Sur, CA 93920; or call (408) 667-2795.

NEPENTHE (3.0 SW) This world famous cliffside restaurant commands stunning views of the Big Sur coast, countryside, and canyons. Lunch, dinner, and cocktails are served in the redwood beamed restaurant and outside. (408) 667-2345.

Owned and operated by the Fassett lineage, generations of other Big Sur families have worked here. See page 51 for a historical perspective on Nepenthe.

CAFE KEVAH (3.0 SW) on the lower level from Nepenthe, takes you one step closer to the continent's edge and serves brunch on the outside patio, starting at 9:00 A.M. 667-2344.

THE PHOENIX SHOP AT NEPENTHE (3.0 SW) Stepping into this treasure house of collections from exotic places around the earth, one almost feels tempted to show a passport. Books, music, clothing, jewelry, and numerous gift and personal items are sold. Kaffe Fassett's renowned knits from London are on display. Open daily, 10:00 A.M. to 6:00 P.M. (408) 667-2457.

HENRY MILLER MEMORIAL LIBRARY (3.3 SE) houses works by and about the famous author, who once resided in Big Sur. See page 51. Phone for hours. (408) 667-2574.

DEETJENS BIG SUR INN (3.8 SE) Unchanged from Grandpa Deetjen's legendary construction of the 1930s, the unique old-world inn of Castro Canyon features Norwegian country charm in its rustic rooms and restaurant. Classical music fills the fireplaced dining cabins where home cooked breakfasts and dinners are served. Operated by the non-profit Deetjen Preservation as a registered historic landmark, the foundation strives to maintain its legacy. Reservations are a must for rooms and dinner. 667-2377, 667-2378.

COAST GALLERY and **COAST CAFE** (6.1 SE) Tucked into Lafler Canyon, antique water tanks house a collection of local and other fine art, a clothing boutique, gift and personal items, its own baker and candlestick maker. Upstairs, the Coast Cafe, overlooking th ocean, serves savory food and beverages from 9:00 A.M. to 5:00 P.M. (408) 667-2301.

The Dark Angel *towers above the Phoenix Shop at the famed Nepenthe Restaurant. Big Sur artist and 40 year resident, Cyril (Bus) Brown sculpted the stunning piece from native redwood and characterized the face with mosaics. In Greek mythology, the dark angel is the death angel who escorts one's soul from this earth.* (Photo by Heidi McGurrin)

As far as the eyes can see, the south coast of Big Sur unfolds in a vast succession of ridges with deep intervening canyons. This wild, tip-tilted region engenders an isolated type of life for its sparse population, with interior portions from Lucia to Salmon Creek existing with no commercial power source.
(Photo by Jim Neill)

The South Coast

TORRE CANYON BRIDGE (7.1 S) spans the broad gorge named for its first inhabitants, the De la Torre family.

DE ANGULO TRAIL (8.1 SE) traverses the steep west side of Partington Ridge, often coming close to very private property on which hikers are most unwelcome. From the turnout on the highway's east side, a wide path ascends some 50 feet to the trail head, which branches off to the left. Don't take the one straight ahead. Cold Springs Camp is four miles in, the Coast Ridge Road is three miles, and eight miles to the south fork of the Big Sur River. Check with USFS at Big Sur Station for current trail conditions. (408) 667-2423.

Jaime de Angulo, a colorful character who lived atop Partington Ridge in the early 1900s, lives on in the legends that circulate about his lifestyle and antics. A descendant of Spanish royalty, he was a Johns Hopkins University honor graduate, an author, and a linguist who spoke more than

30 languages, many of them Indian dialects. See page 45.

PARTINGTON RIDGE (8.3 SE) This sparsely inhabited private community is off limits to the uninvited.

PARTINGTON CANYON AND COVE (9.2 SW) score the northernmost confines of Julia Pfeiffer Burns State Park. Park on the highway's east side, cross the road, and descend the wide trail. The senses awaken to the rhythm of the seaward bound Partington Creek rushing into the canyon, fragrances of the forest, and colorful fauna. At the bottom, the trail straight ahead leads into the redwood canyon. Turn right to follow the creek to its mouth and a small rocky beach.

Partington Cove sits on the other side of the wooden footbridge over the creek and through the 50 foot tunnel. You'll find it mostly unchanged from centuries ago when native Indians launched canoes from the rocky beach

27

just around the point to the north. The small caverns dotting its walls go well with the rumors of this as one of the coast's reputed landings for the smuggling of liquor during Prohibition.

At the trail's end, the rusty fittings of an old Partington Landing launch still exist. In 1874, after hearing of the abundance of tanbark oak and other timber in nearby coastal canyons, John Partington, his wife Laura, and their five children homesteaded surrounding land. They settled on the far side of Partington Ridge, in a sunny little valley, a thousand feet above the sea.

With a partner, he formed a company and built Partington Landing. Try to imagine the activities here, around the turn of the 19th century, when hearty pioneers like Sam Trotter sledded many loads of tanbark down this great canyon for shipment.

Cattle and hides also departed by sea and early residents welcomed provision boats from San Francisco. In the early 1920s, as men first dared to carve Highway One from the face of these craggy mountains, contractors landed equipment here, snaking it up the canyon with a donkey engine.

JULIA PFEIFFER BURNS STATE PARK (11.0 SE) From its entrance at McWay Canyon, the 3,722 acre day use sanctuary extends inland and north to Partington Canyon on both sides of the highway for over two miles. A fee is charged for day use and the four environmental campsites. (408) 667-2315.

The Tanbark, Ewoldsen, and Waterfall Cove trails begin among ancient stands of redwoods in McWay Canyon, through which ocean bound McWay Creek rushes to its fall from Saddle rock. The Waterfall Cove Trail follows it for a short distance before tunneling under the highway.

Along the cliffside trail west of the tunnel, bouquets of California bya laurel and eucalyptus trees permeate the pure air. Splashes of colors from springtime wildflowers are dazzling. However, give the allergenic, shiny-leafed poison oak a wide berth. Beneath the pathway, the canyon's mouth and Waterfall Cove open up to an unsurpassed panorama, climaxed by the time worn Saddle Rock, where McWay Creek plummets over 50 feet into the ocean.

Prior to 1900, the Edward Water's family homesteaded an expanse here, calling it the Saddle Rock Ranch. Next came the McWay family, for whom other landmarks are named. Of these pioneers, perhaps Lathrop and Helen Brown can be most appreciated for donating this land to California for use as a state park.

In 1926, the Brown family purchased Saddle Rock Ranch and eventually built a home opposite the waterfall. Daughter Mimi Brown Jenkins recalls trips by horse and mule along narrow mountain trails and dramatic rides in the funicular which was the only access to the Waterfall House. When friends and neighbors Julia Pfeiffer Burns and her husband made lengthy treks to town from their Slate's Hot Springs home, they often dropped off yeast and animals at the Brown house for safekeeping.

A former New York congressman, Lathrop

The 200-foot long tunnel that leads to Partington Cove was cut through the sheer rock cliff sometime in the 1880's by John Partington and his business partner Bert Stephens as a passageway to the landing where they shipped lumber and fence posts. The six foot wide by eight feet high tunnel is still intact and adds further enhancement to a hike down from the highway to Partington Cove, a part of Julia Pfeiffer-Burns State Park. (Lewis Josselyn Photo from the Pat Hathaway Collection)

"Saddle Rock," at the mouth of McWay Canyon and the adjacent waterfall where McWay Creek plummets over 50 feet into the ocean are beautiful landmarks below the cliffside trail at Julia Pfeiffer-Burns State Park. This waterfall is said to be the only one that falls directly into the sea on the California coast. The Edward Waters family homesteaded this land before the turn of the century and called it the Saddle Rock Ranch after the natural rock landmark. Lathrop and Helen Brown purchased the ranch in the 1930's, built a house out near the rock and an eslator from the highway to the house as a passageway. The Brown's donated their 1700 acres of land to the state for use as a park in the 1960's. (Photo by Jim Neill)

Brown was a close friend to Franklin Roosevelt and served as best man at his wedding. Even so, the house built by Brown at the top of Partington Canyon was not intended as Roosevelt's retirement home, as has been rumored. When the state determined that funds were not available to maintain the Brown home as a museum, as had been stipulated, it was pushed into the ocean.

ANDERSON CANYON (11.8 S) is privately owned and suggests no clues of an 80 year span of history, dawning with the arrival of homesteader Peter Andersen in 1883. In addition to the tanbark operation at Andersen's Landing, the area also hosted a highway road camp for prison workers in the 1930s, and later an artist and Bohemian colony in the abandoned buildings. See pages 47 - 48 AND 50.

SOUTH COAST CENTER (13.2 SE) Not open to the public, this complex primarily houses staff and students from Esalen Institute, a mile to the south.

ESALEN INSTITUTE (14.6 SW) is acknowledged as the world's foremost center for the development of human potential. Co-founder Michael Murphy's book, *The Future of the Body*, published in 1992, addresses in depth many of the subjects pioneered in Esalen workshops. Reservations are essential for these studies and include room, board, and full use of the facilities such as the hot baths and therapeutic massage.

The public's chance to soak in Esalen's "hot, healing waters" under the stars, comes in the early morning hours from one to 3:30 A.M., by

reservation, (408) 667-3047. Sunday to Thursday evenings, established Big Sur residents may use the baths, also for a fee, from 8:00 to 10:00 P.M., by joining the reservation line at the gate house.

Esselen and Salinan Indians, native to this coast for thousands of years, probably bathed in the hot, soothing waters that drain from the cliffs above the ocean here. In the 1860s, Thomas Slate, crippled with arthritis, came here after learning of it from Indians in the Salinas Valley. After soaking repeatedly for several weeks, his symptoms completely disappeared. Convinced, he bought the springs and surrounding land, calling it Slate's Hot Springs.

Around 1910, Dr. and Mrs. H. C. Murphy of Salinas acquired the property. In 1939, following the completion of the coast highway, the Murphy's opened the hot springs as a resort, "Tokitok," an Indian word meaning "hot, healing waters." Later it became known as Big Sur Hot Springs. In the 1960s, son Michael Murphy co-founded Esalen Institute. Phone (408) 667-3000 for information and 667-3049 for an Esalen Bookstore mail order catalogue.

DOLAN CREEK (16.1 S) takes the name of an early settler. Scented eucalyptus trees line the road here.

BIG CREEK BRIDGE (19.1 S) Passing over its double arches, one gains as even greater sense of an expanding coastal wilderness. The 25-acre Big Creek Ranch stretched for four miles along the highway and eastward into the uplands of mountain slopes.

Not open to the public, it is known today

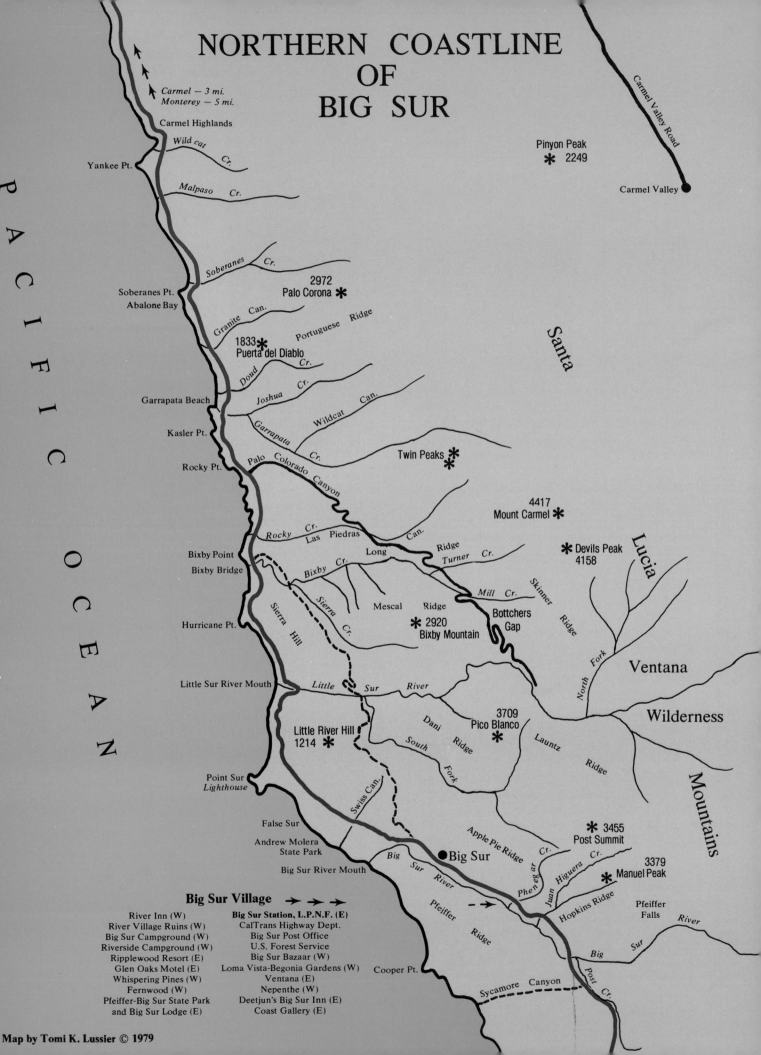

NORTHERN COASTLINE OF BIG SUR

PACIFIC OCEAN

Carmel – 3 mi.
Monterey – 5 mi.

Carmel Highlands

Wild cat Cr.

Yankee Pt.

Malpaso Cr.

Carmel Valley Road

Pinyon Peak
* 2249

Carmel Valley

Soberanes Cr.

Soberanes Pt.
Abalone Bay

Granite Can.

Portuguese Ridge

2972
Palo Corona *

Santa

1833 *
Puerta del Diablo

Doud Cr.

Joshua Cr.

Garrapata Beach

Wildcat Can.

Kasler Pt.

Garrapata Cr.

Twin Peaks *

Rocky Pt.

Palo Colorado Canyon

4417
Mount Carmel *

Rocky Cr.

Las Piedras

Long Can.

Ridge Turner Cr.

* Devils Peak
4158

Lucia

Bixby Point
Bixby Bridge

Bixby Cr.

Mescal Ridge

Mill Cr.

Skinner Ridge

Bottchers Gap

Sierra Cr.

Sierra Hill

* 2920
Bixby Mountain

North Fork

Ventana

Hurricane Pt.

Little Sur River Mouth

Little Sur River

3709
Pico Blanco *

Wilderness

Little River Hill
1214 *

Dani Ridge

South Fork

Launtz Ridge

Point Sur
Lighthouse

Swiss Can.

Mountains

False Sur

Andrew Molera
State Park

Big Sur River Mouth

Apple Pie Ridge

* 3455
Post Summit

Big Sur

Phenegar Cr.

Juan Higuera Cr.

3379
* Manuel Peak

Big Sur River

Pfeiffer Ridge

Hopkins Ridge

Pfeiffer Falls

River

Big Sur Village →→→

River Inn (W)	**Big Sur Station, L.P.N.F. (E)**
River Village Ruins (W)	CalTrans Highway Dept.
Big Sur Campground (W)	Big Sur Post Office
Riverside Campground (W)	U.S. Forest Service
Ripplewood Resort (E)	Big Sur Bazaar (W)
Glen Oaks Motel (E)	Loma Vista-Begonia Gardens (W)
Whispering Pines (W)	Ventana (E)
Fernwood (W)	Nepenthe (W)
Pfeiffer-Big Sur State Park	Deetjun's Big Sur Inn (E)
and Big Sur Lodge (E)	Coast Gallery (E)

Cooper Pt.

Sycamore Canyon

Post Cr.

Big Sur River

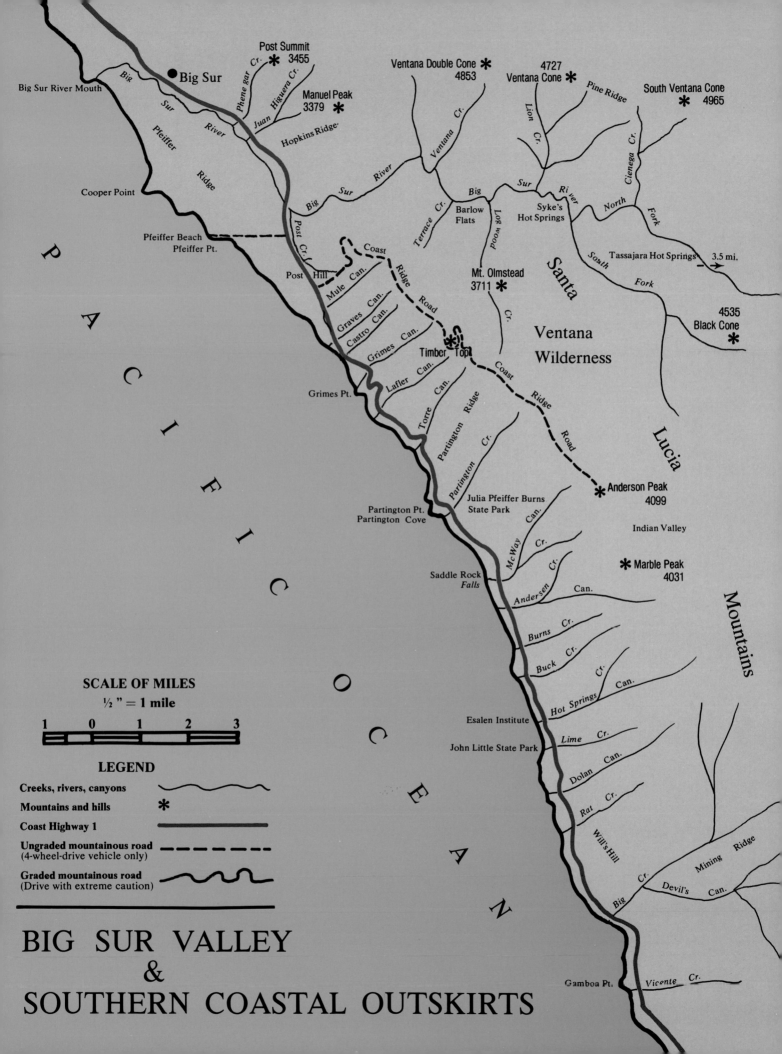

Big Sur River Mouth

Cooper Point

Big Sur

Phene gar Cr.

Post Summit
3455

Higuera Cr.

Juan

Manuel Peak
3379

Hopkins Ridge

Ventana Double Cone
4853

4727
Ventana Cone

Pine Ridge

South Ventana Cone
4965

Big Sur River

Pfeiffer Ridge

Pfeiffer Beach
Pfeiffer Pt.

Post Cr.

Post Hill

Coast

Mule Can.

Graves Can.

Castro Can.

Grimes Can.

Lafler Can.

Torre Can.

Ridge

Road

Timber Top

Partington Ridge

Terrace Cr.

Big

Barlow Flats

Lot wood Cr.

Sur

Ri ver

Syke's
Hot Springs

Cienega Cr.

North Fork

South Fork

Tassajara Hot Springs

3.5 mi.

Lion Cr.

Mt. Olmstead
3711

Santa

Ventana
Wilderness

4535
Black Cone

Coast

Ridge

Road

Grimes Pt.

Partington Cr.

Partington Pt.
Partington Cove

Julia Pfeiffer Burns
State Park

Saddle Rock
Falls

Andersen Cr.

McWay Cr.

Can.

Lucia

Anderson Peak
4099

Indian Valley

Marble Peak
4031

Mountains

Burns Cr.

Buck Cr.

Cr.

Can.

Hot Springs Cr.

Esalen Institute

Lime Cr.

John Little State Park

Dolan Can.

Rat Cr.

Will's Hill

Mining Ridge

Cr.

Devil's Can.

Big Cr.

Gamboa Pt.

Vicente Cr.

PACIFIC OCEAN

SCALE OF MILES

½ " = 1 mile

1   0   1   2   3

LEGEND

Creeks, rivers, canyons

Mountains and hills *

Coast Highway 1

Ungraded mountainous road
(4-wheel-drive vehicle only)

Graded mountainous road
(Drive with extreme caution)

BIG SUR VALLEY
&
SOUTHERN COASTAL OUTSKIRTS

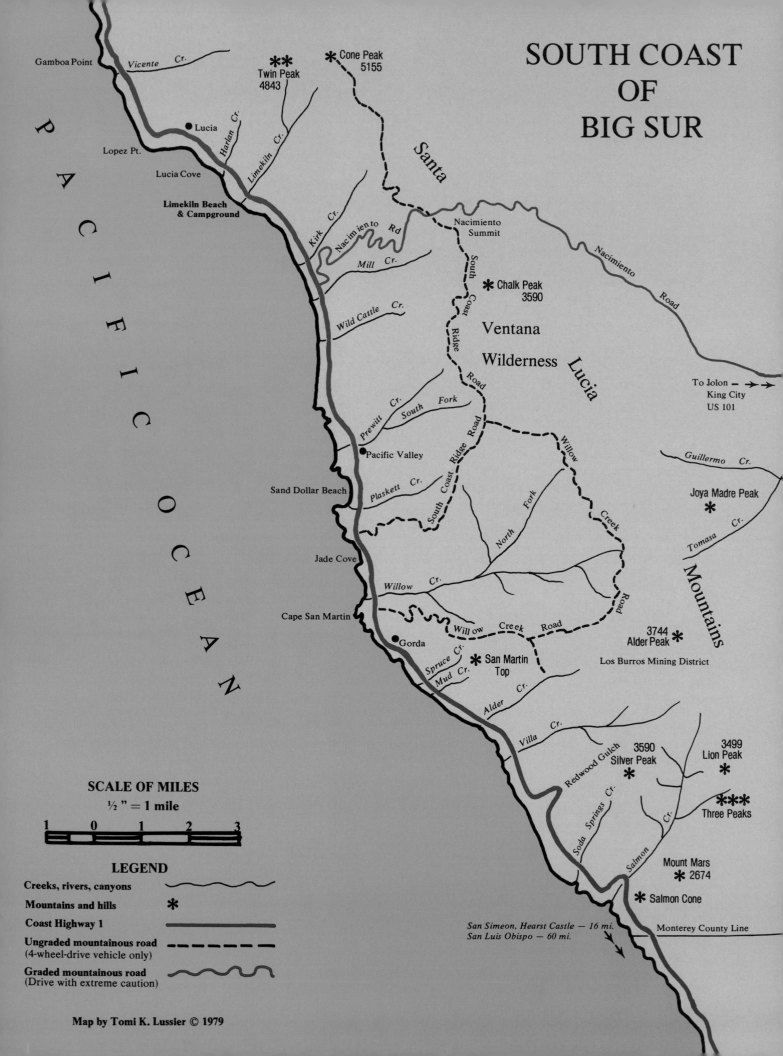

SOUTH COAST
OF
BIG SUR

PACIFIC OCEAN

Gamboa Point
Vicente Cr.

Lucia

Lopez Pt.

Lucia Cove

Limekiln Beach & Campground

Harlan Cr.

Limekiln Cr.

Kirk Cr.

** Twin Peak 4843

* Cone Peak 5155

Santa

Nacimiento Rd

Mill Cr.

Nacimiento Summit

* Chalk Peak 3590

Nacimiento Road

Lucia

To Jolon
King City
US 101

Wild Cattle Cr.

Ventana

Wilderness

South Coast Ridge Road

Prewitt Cr.

South Fork

Pacific Valley

Sand Dollar Beach

Plaskett Cr.

South Coast Ridge Road

North Fork

Willow Creek

Guillermo Cr.

Joya Madre Peak
*

Tomasa Cr.

Jade Cove

Willow Cr.

Cape San Martin

Willow Creek Road

3744
Alder Peak *

Mountains

Gorda

Spruce Cr.

Mud Cr.

* San Martin Top

Creek

Los Burros Mining District

Alder Cr.

Villa Cr.

Redwood Gulch

3590
Silver Peak
*

3499
Lion Peak
*

* * *
Three Peaks

Soda Springs Cr.

Salmon Cr.

Mount Mars
* 2674

* Salmon Cone

San Simeon, Hearst Castle — 16 mi.
San Luis Obispo — 60 mi.

Monterey County Line

SCALE OF MILES
½ " = 1 mile

1   0   1   2   3

LEGEND

Creeks, rivers, canyons

Mountains and hills   *

Coast Highway 1

Ungraded mountainous road
(4-wheel-drive vehicle only)

Graded mountainous road
(Drive with extreme caution)

Map by Tomi K. Lussier © 1979

as the Landels-Hill Big Creek Reserve, and is used by The University of California's Natural Land and Water Reserves system for teaching and research analysis of the wilderness. Many field sciences are studied, including ecology, biology, geology, and archeology. An elite mixture of coastal plants and animals exist. Steelhead run in natural springs and over a hundred species of birds and abundant wildlife have been noted. On the coastline at the mouth of Big Creek, hearty kelp beds and the once threatened sea otters thrive.

In December, 1977, the Landels-Hill Big Creek Reserve was made possible by a partnership of the Nature Conservancy and University of California, assisted by land and monetary donations from private landowners, and a large contribution from the Save the Redwoods League. Ed Landels and Kenneth Hill were principal donors.

The coast's first inhabitants also appreciated this area's abundant resources. Esselen and possibly Salinan Indians lived here over 6,500 years ago, dating back to the early stages of man's settlement in California.

VISTA POINT AT GAMBOA POINT (20.0 S) With its drinking fountains and benches, this pleasurable turnout presents a panorama of the south coast, including the graceful arches of Big Creek Bridge.

LUCIA (24.4 S) is a small south coast community. The prominent Lopez Point nearby can be seen for many miles from south of the Big Sur Valley.

Wilbur Harlan homesteaded an expanse here in 1895, preempted a timber claim, and later acquired more acreage. He married Ada Dani, the community's midwife. Her parents, Gabriel and Elizabeth Dani, had settled on land on the current day New Camaldoli Hermitage. Another daughter, Lucia Dani, christened after the mountain range, became the post mistress and the community took her name.

Harlan children walked a mile to the first redwood schoolhouse, located up the hill from the original homestead. After the highway came through, the school was moved to a spot closer to the road. When no children were left to teach, it was relocated to its current location at Pacific Valley, eight miles to the south.

Folks used to say of the schools on the south coast: "They train a mule to bring in the school teacher. Then they shoot the mule and marry the teacher." At one time, two families of the neighborhood claimed to have accounted for ten teachers.

Most of the time, the ten Harlan children participated in the family's need for self-sufficiency. They gathered eggs, milked cows, canned fruits and vegetables, hunted, fished, and cared for livestock and poultry.

The schoolteacher boarded with them along with other family members, making it quite a clan. A 50 pound sack of flour was made into loaves of bread each week and biscuits from family-raised wheat joined a table often laid out with venison, pork, poultry, fish or seafood. Staples, such as coffee, came by mule trail from King City, 20 miles over the mountains.

Sometimes provisions arrived on a chartered steamer from San Francisco, which would sit offshore of the present day Lucia Lodge in view of the Dani, Gamboa, Avila, Boronda, Lopez, and Harlan families, who had gathered for the auspicious occasion. Wilbur Harlan often brought the coveted items ashore in his homemade rowboat, aided by a cable attached to a rock. The oldest Harlan, riding on a mule, would haul the cargo to its final destination.

Today, some of Wilbur Harlan's descendants continue to live on the land. Harlan Creek meanders across their property and unites with the sea on the south side of Lucia Lodge.

LUCIA LODGE (24.5 SW) Traveling from the north, a convenience store, and restaurant may seem an oasis after 20 miles without benefit of a commercial establishment. Still operated by the Harlan family, the lodge and ten cabins nearby face the ocean. Breakfast, lunch, and dinner are served, featuring California cuisine and locally caught fish from pure waters. The dining deck offers diverse views, including whale watching part of the year. For room reservations, call or write Lucia Lodge, Highway One Lucia; Big Sur, CA 93920. (408) 667-2391.

IMMACULATE HEART HERMITAGE, NEW CAMALDOLI (25.0 SE) A large white cross on the highway's inland side marks the entrance to the self-sufficient community of Camaldolese Monks, who live peacefully, devoting their lives to prayer and meditation. In 1958, three Camaldoli Fathers settled on western slopes of the Lucia Ranch, 1300 feet above the sea, and the New Camaldoli Hermitage was born.

The parent house of the original

In spite of outstanding structural differences the picturesque Big Creek Bridge on the south coast has been repeatedly misidentified as Bixby Bridge on the north coast. Big Creek Bridge crosses the canyon 90 feet above the stream bed and is over 500 feet in length. The completion of this bridge opened the Coast Highway 1 in 1937. In 1977, the 4000-acre Big Creek Ranch that spreads for four miles along the coast and into the uplands of the mountains was purchased by the Nature Conservancy, with the owners of the land first making a generous donation of the purchase price. It will be used as an outdoor laboratory for ecological and biological studies.
(Photo by John Osterman)

mouth. Company schooners delivered barrels of lime to market and boats brought the mail to a nearby post office. Supplies for the isolated residents came by boat and were carried by pack animals over narrow, mountain trails to homes. The Limekiln Point area proposed a challenge to road engineers of the new highway in the early 1930s. Over 163,000 cubic yards of solid rock were removed in only a thousand feet of roadway. Thirty-five tons of dynamite were used in just one blast.

LIMEKILN CREEK REDWOODS CAMPGROUND (26.4 S) offers 65 sites on the beach, creek-side, and among the redwoods. Hiking trails lead into the forest where the old limekilns still stand. (408) 667-2403.

KIRK CREEK AND CAMPGROUND (28.4 S) Operated by the U.S. Forest Service, the 33 campsites and picnic area rest on an open bluff facing the sea.

The Kirk Creek trail begins here on the highway's east side. Climbing the switchbacks, keen ocean views linger for some distance.

NACIMIENTO-FERGUSSON ROAD (28.8 SE) On the south end of Kirk Creek Bridge is the turnout to the only eastern passage road between Carmel and San Simeon. Some of nature's most bountiful productions are staged along the steep, winding strip of mountainous road, offering the unhurried traveler a rare opportunity for an inland jaunt into the back country. Some 50 miles further on, it joins U.S. Highway 101, a major artery between San Francisco and Los Angeles. However, it cannot be considered a short cut, due to the slow approach. Mudslides often close the road in rainy weather.

The chaparral-covered hills are home to hundreds of species of trees, birds, wildflowers and wild animals. Wild boar and black-tailed deer quietly roam the hillsides and graze in meadows, especially in early morning and evening.

An ascent of eight miles lies between Kirk

Camaldolese Order has been located high in the Apennine Mountains of Italy since the year 1012. This small and oldest order of monks was founded by Saint Romuald, who lived according to the teachings of Saint Benedict.

Retreat facilities are open to both men and women for a usual stay of three days. Residents are encouraged, but not required to join in the liturgical services of the community and are asked to maintain the atmosphere of quiet and recollection.

Request reservations in writing to the Guestmaster, IMMACULATE HEART HERMITAGE, New Camaldoli; Big Sur, CA 93920, or call (408) 667-2456.

LIMEKILN CREEK (26.4 S) This area supported a fair-sized community of people in the 1880s, when the Rockland Cement Company operated a prosperous limekiln operation in the canyon and the small port of Rockland Landing at its

Creek and the 4000 foot Nacimiento Summit. The Plaskett Ridge Road, also known as the South Coast Ridge Road, has its northern end here. Only four-wheel-drive vehicles should travel this precarious southbound track, which ends some 12 miles to the south at Highway One near Pacific Valley.

From Nacimiento Summit, heading east, the road descends about three miles to the U.S. Forest Service Nacimiento Campground, located in a peaceful setting among streams, oaks, and madrone at an elevation of 1600 feet. Ponderosa Campground is one mile further on. See page 10 for camping and permit information. King City lies about 35 miles to the east.

From the Ponderosa Campground, Nacimiento Road winds through the Hunter Liggett Military Reservation for about fifteen miles to Mission Road, about five miles west of Jolon. The Hunter Liggett Military Headquarters are nearby.

North of the headquarters, The Mission San Antonio de Padua, in typical early California-Spanish style, is located in the beautiful Valley of the Oaks. In 1771, Father Junipero Serra established this as the third California mission. The public may visit it daily.

King City and U.S. Highway 101 lie twenty miles ahead. Check with the U.S. Forest Service for information about other campgrounds accessible from this area. (408) 385-5434.

MILL CREEK (29.3 S) flows into the ocean alongside a Los Padres National Forest picnic area with a small accessible beach nearby.

PACIFIC VALLEY (32.0 S) From Wild Cattle Creek on the north to Willow Creek on the south, the valley represents an ancient marine terrace about a mile wide and four miles in length. The northernmost section of the Los Burros Mining District occupies a portion of the eastern hills. Renowned for their jade deposits, the area's beaches offer better accessibility than those of the northern coast.

PACIFIC VALLEY CENTER (32.5 SE) is flanked by mountains and ocean and sits on a hillside spotted with gardens of wildflowers. The Wildflower Gift Gallery specializes in these seeds, authentic Indian jewelry, books, and jade. The Chevron gas station also sells diesel fuel. A general store has groceries, an espresso and juice bar, and video rentals. Upstairs, an outside dining deck precedes the cafe which serves breakfast, lunch, dinner, and cocktails. Their chili and apple pie recipes have won local awards. 927-8655.

PACIFIC VALLEY STATION OF LOS PADRES NATIONAL FOREST (33.2 SE) issues permits to hikers entering the Ventana Wilderness trails leading from this area. See page 10.

Lucia Lodge on the south coast sits ashore of the cove of the same name in the small community of Lucia. Lodge guests use kerosene lanterns for lighting when nightfall comes. The community takes its name from a one-time postmistress named Lucia Dani who was herself named for the Santa Lucia Mountain Range.
(Photo by John Osterman)

SAND DOLLAR BEACH AND PICNIC AREA
(35.6 SW) The crescent-shaped, sandy strand is most approachable. The Los Padres Forest facility has rest rooms and fire pits as well.

PLASKETT CREEK CAMPGROUND (36.1 S) Set against the beautiful Santa Lucia Mountains, the 45 sites are administered by the forest service. To the west, Plaskett Point marks the northernmost margin of Jade Cove. The jade found nearby usually lacks the quality and color of that found at the cove's southern end.

SOUTH COAST RIDGE ROAD - PLASKETT RIDGE ROAD (36.5 SE) This four-wheel-drive, dirt road travels in an easterly direction for several miles before arching north over Plaskett ridge. At the entrance, a sign reads: Nacimiento Road - 12 miles, South Coast Ridge Jeep Road - 7 miles, Plaskett Ridge Camp - 6 miles.

JADE COVE (36.8 SW) is marked by a Los Padres National Forest sign. Jade Cove is actually a string of coves, extending from Plaskett Point on the north to Willow Creek on the south. The cove is reached by a short walk through pasture land and a descent along a path to the rocky beach, where 150 foot cliffs surround the cove on three sides. Wave patterns can be unpredictable and dangerous. For some, the Willow Creek beach, a mile south, is safer.

Jade is most readily found at low tide and following winter storms. Wave movements, currents, and tides break up the jade and serpentine that exists in the solid rock beneath the surface and serpentine ledges in the ocean. Nephrite jade, one of the two true varieties, is found here and is usually the rare blue-green color. Black jade, a mixture of black and green, can also be found.

To identify a genuine piece of nephrite jade, any algae or material on the rock must be scraped or washed away. Jade has a dull, waxy, or pearly appearance, but after dipping it in water or shining by rubbing it against the side of your nose, the stone takes on an oil glow. Whether wet or dry, it feels soapy when rubbed. It is harder than steel and can be tested with a knife. Usually green, it also occurs in a variety of colors.

In 1971, three divers brought up a 9,000 pound jade boulder after working for months at 30 feet beneath the surface on its removal. Over eight feet in length, this magnificent piece was valued at $180,000. *Jade Beneath the Sea, A Diving Adventure,* a book written by one of the divers, describes the operation and is sold at Pacific Valley's Wildflower Gift Gallery.

WILLOW CREEK (38.4 S) A road on the south side leads down to Willow Creek beach, a picnic area, and rest rooms.

Heavy surf often washes into this area at the southernmost side of Jade Cove. Jade is found on the beach, especially at low tide, and some small pieces are sometimes deposited in the bed of Willow Creek that runs into the ocean here. Plaskett Rock, a large offshore sea stack stands to the north.

CAPE SAN MARTIN (38.7 SW) is the rock promontory south of Willow Creek. An automatic navigational light atop the cape can be seen for miles by mariners at sea.

WILLOW CREEK ROAD (38.9 SE) This precarious dirt road requires a four-wheel-drive or sturdy vehicle. A sign at the entrance reads: Willow Creek Spring Camp - 4 miles, Alder Creek Camp - 9 miles, and Three Peaks Camp - 20 miles.

Over a century ago, it was merely a donkey trail leading to the active Los Burros Mining District. A thousand mining claims were filed from 1870 to 1890.

W.D. Cruikshank's discovery of gold southeast of Pacific Valley in 1887, prompted an influx of people near Cruikshank's "Last Chance Mine," creating the boom town of Manchester, named for a cantankerous, hard-hitting blacksmith. Obviously, he didn't hit hard enough, because it was renamed Mansfield in 1889. Its population of 300 once supported five saloons, a dance hall, confectionery, two general stores, and a restaurant. Supplies were hauled in by pack train from Jolon, over the mountains to the east. Occasionally, provisions were delivered by boat at the mouth of Willow Creek on the coast and packed in by mules.

By 1895 most of the available gold, copper, and silver were depleted and the area's remoteness made mining unprofitable. Slowly, activity declined and the town became another coastal legend after in burned around the turn of the 19th century. Mining claims for various minerals are still worked in the Los Burros District, from the northern border at Plaskett Ridge to San Carpojo Creek. As one example, evidence of the prodigious mineral deposits of these mountains can be traced through history to the large limestone deposits at Bixby Canyon, Pico Blanco, and Limekiln Canyon.

WILLOW SPRINGS HIGHWAY MAINTENANCE STATION (39.7 SE) The Caltrans crew here maintains the especially rugged southern section of Highway One.

GORDA (39.9 S) is the last stop on the Big Sur mailman's route, prompting many to think of it as Big Sur's southern border. In 1932, residents established the 20-acre community and named it after Gorda Rock, an offshore sea stack that resembles a fat lady. Gorda is a Spanish word for "fat."

The annual Gorda Jade Festival is held the first weekend of October. Local jade, rock, and wood creations are displayed and sold in booths, along with similar remarkable items from far away places.

GORDA'S LODGING (39.9 SE) consists of four small houses that overlook the ocean in a quiet setting. (805) 927-4588.

GORDA GENERAL STORE (39.9 SE) is a full service market with movie rentals and camping supplies. (805) 927-3918

SOUTH COAST CAFE AND BAKERY (39.9 SE) features locally caught fish and dishes up home styled breakfasts, lunches, dinners on weekends, and fresh pastries. (805) 927-1950.

GORDA GAS STATION (39.9 SE) sells BP gas. (805) 927-8971.

BIG SUR JADE COMPANY (39.9 SE) sells mostly local jade jewelry and carvings, and fills custom orders. A self-made, six foot, diamond dredge saw carves through boulders. An undisputed jade master conducts hunting and teaching tours. (805) 927-8971.

LOS PADRES NATIONAL FOREST PICNIC AREA AND REST ROOMS AT GORDA (39.9 SW) Thank the California State Coastal Conservancy for this 24 acre oceanside preserve.

SALMON CREEK (48.1 S) The lengthy hairpin curve here at 770 feet offers as much drama as most people care to endure. The redwood belt of *Sequoia sempervirens* begins north of the California state line and ends right here, with a small stand of redwoods in a side gulch of Salmon Creek.

A number of Los Padres National Forest hiking trails lead from this area. Check in at the Salmon Creek Station nearby for possible permits. See page 10.

MONTEREY-SAN LUIS OBISPO COUNTY LINE (50.1 S) As you cross the southern border of Monterey County, the distance to San Simeon is 16 miles, Morro Bay - 48 miles, San Luis Obispo - 60 miles, and Los Angeles - 260 miles.

RAGGED POINT INN (51.6 SW) has 19 ocean view rooms, a carry-out sandwich shop, Union 76 gas, and a nature trail leading to the beach. Box 110, San Simeon, CA 93452. (805) 927-4502.

SAN CARPOJO CREEK (53.3 S) For the first time in many miles, you're close to sea level.

HEARST CASTLE (66.1 SE) sprawls about an enchanted hill in San Simeon. For 28 years newspaper publisher William Randolph Hearst, who was portrayed in the movie classic *Citizen Kane*, supervised the creation of his dream estate of 165 rooms and 127 acres of gardens and terraces. The castle houses his renowned collection of European art and antiques.

Daily tours of the state historic monument depart by bus from the visitor center and are almost two hours in length. Reservations can be made by phone to Mistix at (800) 444-7275, purchased directly at Mistix ticket offices within a 50 mile radius of the Castle, or from the monument's ticket office.

Lodging for castle guests may be obtained from San Simeon's Chamber of Commerce, (805) 927-3500 or the Cambria Chamber of Commerce, (805) 927-3624.

Hearst History

Midway between San Francisco and Los Angeles, Hearst Castle stands as the most majestic private home ever constructed in America. Here, William Randolph Hearst created an elaborate and colossal shrine to art and beauty.

Born in San Francisco in 1863, "Willie" was the only child of millionaire, miner, and rancher, George Hearst and Phoebe Apperson Hearst. From both parents, he inherited a love of art, beauty, and nature. Even as a child, he accompanied one or both parents on art and antique buying trips to Europe.

One of George Hearst's favorite real estate acquisitions was the 3,000 acre Santa Rosa Ranch in the Santa Lucia Mountains that faced the bay of San Simeon. The Mission of San Miguel Arcangel had originally owned most of the area. In 1834, Mexico secularized the missions, divided the land, and gave it to influential citizens. Some of it was sold to the earliest real estate brokers. Hearst bought the ranch from the Estrada family. Later, Senator George Hearst accumulated some 45,000 acres after adding the adjoining ranches of Piedra Blanca and San Simeon.

In summer months, he and young Willie would take a train to Paso Robles where their party would be met by vaqueros and transported on horseback to San Simeon. Occasionally, Hearst and friends made the sojourn from Monterey over the tortuous trails of the mountains. After he build a wharf at San Simeon in 1878, father, mother, and son would arrive aboard a steamer from San Francisco.

In 1887, George Hearst gave his son the *San Francisco Examiner.* Thus, at the age of 23, William Randolph Hearst launched a career that was to make him a legendary publisher and the creator of America's second great fortune. Between 1895 and 1920, W. R. Hearst procured thirty newspapers, over a dozen magazines, eight radio stations, and several film companies.

Architect Julia Morgan was the first woman graduate of the Beaux Arts School in Paris. She claimed Phoebe Hearst as a dear friend. Following Mrs. Hearst's death in 1919, William R. Hearst and Miss Morgan began an architectural odyssey at San Simeon.

Already, warehouses were bulging with his collections of carved ceilings, mantlepieces, medieval castles and other art objects. For over fifty years, Hearst spent over a million dollars a year on art and antiques. Miss Morgan always asserted that Hearst was the real architect of the ranch, claiming that her contribution had been technical.

Today, many wild animals, including zebra, roam the hills, Hearst's original private zoo and game reserve remains unequaled. Among the many species that once caroused a 2,000 acre enclosure were a great variety of lions, wildcats, cheetahs, spotted leopards, monkeys, an orangutan, eagles, cockatoos, a black panther, and an elephant. White polar bears from the Arctic joined black bears from Alaska. Bison and zebras, llamas and spotted deer meandered about the ranch.

Ultimately, the ranch encompassed 275,000 acres. It covered over 50 miles of coastline into Monterey County and spread north to the Mission San Antonio de Padua at Jolon. After the outbreak of World War II, Hearst sold 140,000 acres to the government for the Hunter Liggett Military Reservation.

In August, 1951, America's greatest art collector and publisher died, leaving a legacy of splendor and fulfilled dreams. The state received the castle in June, 1958.

The California Division of Highways encountered special problems in the construction of the magnificent Bixby Bridge. Placing a 320-foot arch over the V-shaped canyon with its 100 foot wide bottom was quite an engineering feat. The 260 foot height of the bridge, length of the span, and high winds and wave action at the construction site added to an already challenging job. Lumber and cement was shipped by rail to Monterey, over 20 miles to the north, and then trucked along a one-way hazardous winding dirt road. Sand and rock aggregate was obtained from a screening plant set up at the mouth of the Big Sur River, eight miles to the south. The movement and handling of forms, falsework material and concrete was by way of cable, usually ridden by a workman simply holding onto the cable that was strung across the canyon over 300 feet in the air. Construction on the concrete placings of the approach spans began November 3, 1931, but construction of the arch did not begin until the following spring when the danger of high winds had passed. This photograph was taken May 23, 1932, six months before its dedication. One construction alternative considered by engineers was the use of steel instead of concrete. The most dramatic alternative would have turned the highway up Bixby Creek several hundred feet to a shorter bridge crossing, sending the highway through a 900 foot tunnel cut through a nearby ridge. (Lewis Josselyn Photo from the Pat Hathaway Collection)

BIG SUR HISTORY

How It All Began:

One need not be a geologist to realize that some of nature's greatest forces combined to form this unusual region. The energy behind these forces is as great in our time as it was millions of years ago, yet our brief stay on earth is not long enough to make one realize that changes are still taking place.

Over 200 million years ago a solid mass of sedimentary rocks accumulated in the area, most of it below sea level. Sometime later these

rocks were taken over by molten (liquid) rock which crystallized. Today these rocks are known as the Sur Series Gneiss and Santa Lucia Granite, respectively, two of the major rock formations of the Santa Lucia Mountains.

Evidence shows that ten to fifteen million years ago the Big Sur coastline was several miles east of the present-day shoreline. Probably ten million years ago the area was locally elevated. Thrust faulting (strong forces causing cracks in the earth's surface) continued, along with westward tilting, and was followed by a series of vertical uplifts, which elevated the main portion of the Santa Lucia Mountain Range as much as 3000 to 5000 feet during Pleistocene and Recent time (1 million to 25,000 years ago).

During this time loose material from the upper slopes was being washed down on the shelves by rains. In some places the shelves were eroded by streams which followed some of the cracks, as can be seen at the mouth of Garrapata Creek. As the long, deep gash leaves the beach and heads southeasterly far back into the mountains, it makes gaps in the ridges it crosses. This may be observed from the highway at Palo Colorado Canyon, upper Rocky Creek, Bixby Creek and the Little Sur River and its branches.

The Big Sur River has been flowing in the region for over a million years, at one time running westward from the gorge area in the Pfeiffer-Big Sur State Park. An older, higher course of the river is in evidence up to 300 feet above the present stream level. Recent uplifts have caused it to cut deeper into its channel, leaving its tell-tale gravel deposits behind.

The Original Inhabitants

The predominant Indians of Big Sur, a small
tribe called the Esselens, once occupied settlements along the coast from Point Sur to the small
community of Lucia, twenty-five miles to the
south. Small villages and campsites of Esselen
inhabitants existed in the Santa Lucia Mountains as far as ten to fifteen miles east of the coastline. They also controlled the upper watersheds
of the Carmel and Arroyo Seco rivers.

The Sargenta-Ruc (eagle-house) nation of the
Costanoan triblet occupied land south of Palo Colorado Canyon to the mouth of the Big Sur River.
Villages of the Sargenta-Ruc existed at Bixby
and Rocky creeks.

The Big Sur coast south of Lucia was home to
the coastal villages of Salinan Indians, although
the majority lived in the Hunter-Ligget area and
the Salinas Valley.

It is known that the Esselen Indians were in
the Big Sur Valley area at least 3,000 years ago,
some 1000 years B.C. The Monterey County Archaelogical Society established this by radiocar-
bon dating on charcoal samples taken from an
Indian burial site on the Post Ranch on the southern end of the valley.

The diet of the coastal Indians consisted of a-
corns, rabbit, deer, and bear meat, as well as sea
lion, seal, and mollusks. A tule balsa raft was
used by the Indians for fishing in the ocean lagoons, and they most certainly fished along the
banks of the Big Sur River.

Slate's Hot Springs (today's Esalen Institute), and Tassajara Hot Springs (in the Santa
Lucia Mountains east of Big Sur) were used by
the Indians.

The coastal Indians of Monterey County
were brought under the control of the Spanish
missions when New Spain (Mexico) took control
of California in 1770. The mission San Carlos de
Boromeo in Monterey (later moved to Carmel)
Christianized, clothed, and acculturated the Indians towards the Hispanic mode. Thus the population estimates of the Big Sur Indians, as well
as other particulars, come from the old mission
records.

The estimated Esselen population from 1770
to 1803 was probably between 900 and 1300, as
assessed by Don Howard of the Monterey County
Archaelogical Society. The population estimates
for the Costanoan and Salinan Indians are somewhat more, but these tribes did not abide exclu-
sively in the Big Sur area.

Extinction of the Big Sur Indians soon came
about as the result of intermarriage that was encouraged by the Spanish and the diseases introduced to them for which they had little natural
resistance. When the first settlers arrived in Big
Sur, the native Indians of the coast were gone.

In the late 1760's Alta California (today's California) was a part of New Spain (Mexico). The land had been explored, but not settled. The primitive Indians were the unchallenged inhabitants of California, that is, until King Charles III of Spain heard that a number of Russians had been seen in Monterey Bay, thirty miles north of Big Sur.

The Russians actually were only after the skin of the populous sea otter of the California coast, which brought fantastic prices on the China trade market. A single pelt might sell for as much as $1700. The Russians hunted the sea otters until they were nearly extinct.

Military expeditions by land and sea were sent out of Mexico by King Charles. Captain Gaspar de Portola led an expedition into California and there is evidence that some men from this expedition were the first non-Indians ever to cross the Santa Lucia Mountains and the coastline of Big Sur. The year was 1769.

Forts were built by the Spanish to protect the coast, and Father Junipero Serra matched each one with a mission. The Spanish settlement of California had begun and Monterey was declared the capital.

In 1823 Captain John Roger Cooper, a citizen of the United States from Boston, sailed into Monterey Bay with his ship *The Rover*, which the Spanish governor at the time quickly bought in order to bolster the economy of California. He wanted to use the ship for transporting the valuable sea otter pelts to China, and he in turn hired Cooper to command the ship and head the operation. Cooper became a Catholic, was naturalized and married General Vallejo's sister. His half-brother, Thomas Larkin became the American consul in Monterey.

Although the original 8,949-acre land grant of Rancho El Sur in Big Sur was first given to Cooper's nephew, Juan Bautista Alvarado in 1834, Cooper acquired it soon thereafter. The Rancho El Sur extended from the Little Sur River mouth on the northern end, and south to the present day Cooper Point. It extended inland for several miles.

The area at the northern end of the Big Sur Valley was an active cattle ranch even though Cooper continued to live in Monterey, occasionally visiting his ranch house in the Little Sur River valley with his family. The northern section of the ranch became known as the Cooper Ranch; the southern section later became known as the Molera Ranch.

Rancho El Sur remained in the family until 1965, when Frances Molera, Cooper's granddaughter, donated a portion of the land as a state park in honor of her brother, Andrew Molera, who was a popular figure in earlier days in Big Sur.

The other Spanish land grant on the Big Sur Coast, the Rancho San Jose y Sur Chiquito, consisted of 8,875 acres and extended south from the Carmel River to Palo Colorado Canyon. This ranch changed hands a number of times and today this section of the once barren coast has at least two fair-sized subdivisions and a few more "mini-divisions."

In 1846 the United States took possession of California and the Spanish regime ended. Shortly thereafter the coast of Big Sur was open to preemption. Preemption stated that anyone could settle on 160 acres of public land provided that he produced a crop and kept the land in good condition. A purchase price of $1.25 an acre had to be paid within a year. In 1862 the Homestead Act was passed by Congress which said much the same as preemption except that no purchase price had to be paid.

The first settler to the Big Sur Valley was a man named Davis who settled on the Big Sur River. Manuel Innocenti, a former Santa Barbara Mission Indian and later, head vaquero at the Cooper Rancho El Sur, rode through in the 1850's and bought the place from Davis. Others soon followed. Some of them came over the mountains from the Salinas Valley when they were forced out by severe droughts in 1863, 1864, and again in the early 1870's. Others came because they recognized the opportunity to live in a bounteous land and didn't mind the difficulties and hard work involved as a result of Big Sur's isolation. A few, enroute to other places, simply ended up here, were forced to stay because of winter storms and then after becoming attached to the beautiful country, made it a home.

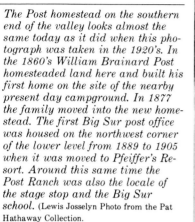

The Post homestead on the southern end of the valley looks almost the same today as it did when this photograph was taken in the 1920's. In the 1860's William Brainard Post homesteaded land here and built his first home on the site of the nearby present day campground. In 1877 the family moved into the new homestead. The first Big Sur post office was housed on the northwest corner of the lower level from 1889 to 1905 when it was moved to Pfeiffer's Resort. Around this same time the Post Ranch was also the locale of the stage stop and the Big Sur school. (Lewis Josselyn Photo from the Pat Hathaway Collection.

These first homesteaders were a noble group of hardworking pioneers. They lived in Big Sur without the advantage of a decent road, electricity, or modern conveniences. They had to be self-sufficent in every sense of the word. Upon arrival they had to cut trees and boards in order to build a house and barn. Crops had to be planted and their ranges had to be supplied with livestock. Hunting wasn't a sport, it was a necessity. Deer meat was often served at meals as well as fish and seafood. Supplies such as staples were brought to the residents twice a year by a coast steamer, which would sit offshore at the Big Sur River mouth, or at other such landings on the coast. Small rowboats would then be used to bring the goods to shore. Another way of getting supplies was a long trip to "town." Monterey was "town" to the residents of the valley and north coast, and King City, twenty miles over the mountains, was "town" to the south coast residents. Many natural dangers existed, including fire, the terrible winter storms, and the wildlife such as the great black eagle and mountain lions, which constantly assaulted the stock. Until the 1880's the fierce grizzly bears further enhanced the threat.

These early pioneers depended on each other quite a bit. Huge social gatherings brought folks from miles around and could go on all night and into the next day. The entire family was packed up on horseback or in wagons to attend the gala events where lots of food, and dancing to the sound of the accordian, banjo, guitar, and violin, set the mood. Christmas, branding time, and the coming of a ship with supplies often instigated such a gathering of friends and neighbors.

Until 1872, when Charlie Bixby and other settlers built a wagon road as far south as Bixby Canyon, there was only a horsetrail leading down the coast. At first the County Board of Supervisors refused assistance for the building of the wagon road because they said "no one would ever live in that country." In 1889, an estimate of the worth of the roads constructed in the area by its industrious pioneers exceeded $15,000. By the 1880's a narrow, winding wagon road meandered as far south as Castro Canyon, located on the southern end of the Big Sur Valley.

In 1853, the mining and panning of gold was going on in the mountains southeast of Big Sur. In 1875, the Los Burros Mining District was formed as a government for the miners who had flocked there. Quantities of gold, silver, and copper were being stripped from the earth. In 1877, the *Last Chance Mine* of Willie Cruikshank at the head of Alder Creek produced huge amounts of gold. This event caused a boom in the population of the district, in spite of its remoteness. Read more about this short-lived gold rush on page 38.

In 1899 the Point Sur Lighthouse was raised atop the "Big Rock," following a number of shipwrecks along the rugged Big Sur coast.

Local ranchers constructed the lighthouse, buildings, and 395 wooden steps that first led up the eastern side of the rock to the top. Kerosene oil powered the first light and a pendulum rotated the lens. Today the rock is uninhabited and the light is operated by computer. See pages 17 and 20 for more information about Point Sur.

Tourism made its debut in Big Sur around the turn of the century. The early tourists to Big Sur reached their destinations by way of stage or horse along the old craggy wagon road which traversed the precipitous mountain slopes of the Santa Lucia. The Southern Pacific Railroad brought the travelers from various parts of the state to Monterey, where the stage would then take them on the ten-hour sojourn to Big Sur.

A tourist fishing resort called the Hotel Idlewild existed on the south fork of the Little Sur River, about a mile east of the present day highway bridge. Guests could elect to stay at the hotel for a rate of $1.50 a day, or in tents that were set up on platforms by the river or in the

In 1889 when work first began on the Point Sur Light, there was not even a road up the cliffside of the "Big Rock." Pack animals and a tramway pulled the building materials for the stone light tower and other structures atop the rock. The Fresnel lens (named for the French physicist who designed it) was brought around the Cape the same year and placed in the tower. At first a pendulum rotated the lens. In 1972 it was replaced by a modern electronic beacon connected to a remote control system at the U.S. Coast Guard Station in Monterey. In 1978 the original lens was disassembled and is now on public display at the Knight Maritime Museum in Monterey.
(Lewis Josselyn Photo from the Pat Hathaway Collection)

redwoods for a rate of $2.00 a week. The resort was frequented by families and nature lovers who reveled in the camping, hiking and fishing at Idlewild. It was said to be a favorite spot of artists, writers, botanists, and photographers who probably found inspiration in the fresh mountain and sea air. Idlewild burned to the ground around 1910, after which another resort by the same name was built on the north fork of the little river. It ceased operation shortly thereafter.

The Pfeiffer Ranch Resort was the first resort in the Big Sur proper. Florence Pfeiffer, the wife of John Pfeiffer, who donated the present day park land, ran the resort from 1908 until 1934 when it was taken over by the park service. Her guests were called to meals in the rose covered, open-air dining porch by a brass dinner bell that was salvaged from the wreck of the ship *Majestic* on the rugged coast. Florence Pfeiffer's guests were nature lovers, artists, writers, Stanford professors, folks just passing through, and out of towners who were there to attend one of the huge Big Sur community gatherings. The names of Robinson Jeffers and George Sterling embellished the guest book.

Around this same time, **Jaime de Angulo,** a colorful character in Big Sur history, operated a "resort" at the top of Partington Ridge called *El Ranchito Los Posares,* the "ranch of sorrows." His brochure describing the retreat let his potential visitors know in no uncertain terms that this was not the place for the tenderfoot. It described the cook at the resort as "crazy." The main lodge consisted of one big room, with a cooking pot in the middle. At bedtime the visitor chose a corner of the room, put down his sleeping bag, and went to sleep.

45

Big Sur Industry Around the Turn of the Century

The smelting of lime in Bixby Canyon gave quite a boost to the population and economy of Big Sur around the turn of the century. In 1906 Charles Bixby sold his lime rich land to the Monterey Lime Company who built kilns up the canyon on Long Ridge above Bixby Creek. After smelting the lime was transported by aerial cable in buckets along a tramway ridden by workmen to Bixby Landing on the coast where it was sent down an extended chute to the company boat below. Eventually the lime was depleted, the heavy rains and winter storms of 1910 brought the lime operation to a halt, and the once bustling settlement at Bixby Canyon was added to the list of abandoned "boom towns" of the west coast. (Lime Kilns — S.L. Slevin Photo; Bixby Point — Lewis Josselyn Photo; Pat Hathaway Collection)

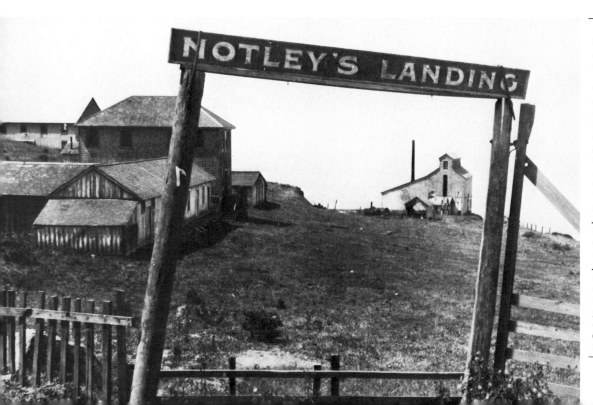

When this photograph was taken in 1919 Notley's Landing was remindful of an Old West ghost town. Today, no buildings remain on the site just south of the mouth of Palo Colorado Canyon where this thriving village centered around the milling and shipping of redwood and tanbark. From 1903 to 1907 the area bustled with activity as ships waited in the tiny cove to take on lumber or bark, sent down from the landing to the boat by way of a long chute. The sound of laughter and music often filled the night air from the tiny dance hall on the cliffside at Notley's where ranchers and workmen gathered for socializing and merriment.
(S.L. Slevin from the
Pat Hathaway Collection)

Industry was introduced to Big Sur in a big way in the late 1880's when the natural resources of tanbark, split redwood, and lime caused a boom of employment along the coast.

The tanbark was valued for its high concentration of tannic acid, which is used for tanning, dyeing, inks, and astringents. The bark was carried out of the canyons on mules over narrow trails. Redwood was in demand for pickets and slabs for furniture, and along with live oak was milled and transported in the same manner. Once out of the canyon, the wood was hauled to one of the landings on the coast, and sent down a chute to the waiting boat. Such landings existed at Notley's, Bixby Point, Big Sur River mouth, Partington Cove, Anderson Creek, and Saddle Rock where the present day Julia Pfeiffer-Burns State Park is located.

It has been estimated that more than 40 million feet of redwood was available in the canyons of Big Sur in those days. At least 50,000 cords of tanbark were shipped out.

Lime was smelted in Bixby Canyon and Limekiln Canyon, which was also known as Rockland Landing. (See page 15 for more information about the lime operation at Bixby Canyon.)

The settlements at Notley's, Bixby's, and the Ventana Power Company, where electric power was generated by the Big Sur River, were quite a boost to the population of the area. However, once these money-making operations came to a halt, the population once again diminished.

In 1918, Lester Gibson, state highway engineer, led a pack train into the Santa Lucia Mountains to make the first location survey for the proposed road that we know today as the Cabrillo Highway, or Highway 1. Other equipment was brought in by launches that landed at various beaches along the coast.

The efforts of the late Dr. John Roberts of Monterey brought about this much-needed highway. In 1897 he had made a five-day trip on foot to map the area. He had figured that the coastal highway could be constructed for $50,000. In 1915 he appeared before the state senate at the request of Senator Rigdon to help convince the legislators of the need for this highway.

The boat Convenva *takes on a load of tanbark at Partington Landing around the turn of the century. The tanbark was brought out of the nearby canyons in "go-devils," logging sleds with wheels on the front and rails on the back, pulled by pack animals. Once out of the steep canyons the bark was brought through the two hundred foot long tunnel on the east side of the cove and out to the landing for shipping.*
(Pat Hathaway Collection)

In 1919 the first highway bonds were voted. In 1922, contracts were awarded and work was started on the new road, with one group working its way north from San Simeon and the other south from Big Sur.

In 1928, convict labor camps were established at the Little Sur River and then moved south to Anderson Canyon. Convicts, along with a number of Chinese, worked as manual laborers on the highway. With good behavior, a convict was allowed to work on the road for a gross wage not to exceed $2.50 a day, with a number of deductions coming out of it. The rules said that he could earn no more than seventy-five cents a day net. His prison time was reduced three days for every two days of work on the road. The prison road camps were honor camps; no uniforms were worn and the guards did not carry guns.

In the 1920's and 30's the famous poet Robinson Jeffers, who had moved to Carmel in 1914, wrote narrative poems about the splendid Big Sur coast and the ranchers who lived there. The tourists mistook Jeffers' characters for the actual residents of the coast and often went knocking on doors of ranch houses to ask questions. This period has been referred to as the time of the "Jeffers' Influence." His influence did help make this part of the central coast famous by the writing of such poems as *Women at Point Sur, Roan Stallion, Mara,* and *Tamar.* He loved the Big Sur country and often camped in the hills. In January of 1962, Jeffers died, not far from this country he had epitomized.

In 1934, John M. Pfeiffer, the son of the original Pfeiffer pioneer, donated a portion of his homesteaded land and sold more acreage for use as a park. Today, Pfeiffer-Big Sur State Park attracts thousands of visitors each year.

In 1934 the school bus started transporting Big Sur young folks of middle and high school age to school in Monterey. Prior to this time, these young men and women had to live in Monterey with friends or relatives to attend high school. Even today, after completion of the sixth grade at the Captain Cooper Grammar School in the valley, young residents travel over seventy miles round trip a day to school in Carmel.

In February of 1935, the Navy's air-ship, the *Macon*, went down near Point Sur when a strong gust of wind disintegrated a portion of the dirigible. The *Macon* drifted out of sight in distress, crash landed, and went down some ten miles to the south. A quick rescue saved all but two members of its eighty-one man crew.

Robinson Jeffers narrates this event in his poem *Mara*, and represents the airship as the *Atlanta*.

In June of 1937, Highway 1 was officially opened by a ribbon cutting ceremony after almost twenty years in the making (due to a lack of funds). The total cost for construction was ten million dollars; eight and a half million over the first appropriation in 1919. Prior to the official designation of the highway as the Cabrillo Highway, it was referred to as the Carmel-San Simeon section of the Roosevelt International Roadway. Today it is known more freely as Highway 1, or Coast Highway 1.

The highway travels a distance of 136 miles between Monterey and San Luis Obispo, but the Big Sur portion takes in 93 miles between Carmel and San Simeon. Over twenty bridges span creeks and canyons of the Big Sur coast between Malpaso Creek, south of Carmel and the southern Monterey County line.

The new highway is six miles shorter than the old county road between Big Sur and Carmel. To the old timer, the new highway meant going to town once a week instead of three or four times a year. Most of the Big Sur folks were not overjoyed with the highway. First of all, they felt that their land had been raped by the landscape. They also felt that hoards of people would come through and commercialization would begin. Land prices would go up and so, as a result, would their property taxes. This, for most, was the biggest problem. Coast residents had very little money to spend — land, yes, but money, no. The advent of the highway was a turning point in the lives of the early Big Sur residents, and changes were yet to come.

In 1937 when the Coast Highway 1 was officially opened, advertisements by real estate and investment companies such as the following ran in the Monterey newspaper: "Sunshine, scenery,

When this photograph was taken in 1927, Bixby Bridge was not yet built and the highway was not completed. Travelers had to take the Old Coast Road to and from Big Sur, beginning on the north side of Bixby Canyon and continuing twelve miles over the mountains in a series of switchbacks. Prior to the completion of the Coast Highway 1, a trip to Big Sur from Monterey took the better part of a day. (Lewis Josselyn Photo from the Pat Hathaway Collection)

views, water, all in 30 minutes time from Monterey. Cabin sites as low as $100; acreage from $25 up. We are also agents for Partington Canyon properties, a high class residential subdivision about 40 miles from Monterey — on the highway with a magnificent view."

Since 1860, the sea otter was thought to be extinct, after the Russians and Spanish had nearly hunted them out. Their gradual reappearance was being monitored by the California Department of Fish and Game as early as the late 1920's. The public, unaware of the return of the sea otter, felt a significant event happened in 1938, when a local couple standing on Bixby Bridge spotted a herd of sea otters foraging for food in the surf. Since that time, the playful "Colonel Blimp" otters have returned to the coastal shores in moderate numbers, and are protected by law.

In 1939, Dr. H.C. Murphy opened a new resort at Slate's Hot Springs on the south coast. He called the resort *Tok-i-tok*, an Esselen Indian word which means "hot healing water." Today this resort is the Esalen Institute, a revolutionary learning and research center in the fields of psychiatry and psychology.

Even though the new highway opened the doors of the once inaccessible Big Sur to the world in 1937, an isolated way of life continued for the residents. Little traffic passed through Big Sur during World War II because gas rationing prevented excessive traveling.

When the war ended, a number of artists, writers and early bohemians migrated to Big Sur in search of isolation and inspiration. The abandoned highway construction shacks at Anderson Creek that had once housed the convict labor provided temporary rent-free housing for many. Anderson Canyon soon became the hub of the gathering art group's activities.

Jean Varda, well known among the San Francisco art group for his unique collages and paintings, first acquainted himself with Big Sur in the early 1940's. Varda told others about the inspiring locale of Big Sur, among them sculptor Benny Bufano and writer Henry Miller, whose books *Tropic of Cancer* and *Tropic of Capricorn* were banned in the United States at the time.

This redwood cabin was built in 1925 by Sam Totter for members of the Pacific Trails Club who enjoyed hiking in the Big Sur hills and surrounding mountains. Later, many of club members built their own homes in Coastlands and on Partington Ridge and the cabin was sold. In 1944 Orson Welles bought the property and in 1947 sold it to Lolly and Bill Fassett who constructed the famous Nepenthe restaurant around the cabin. The Fassett family still owns and operates the unique restaurant that has become known worldwide. The oak tree to the left of the cabin graced the outdoor dining deck of Nepenthe until a few years ago when it died and was replaced by Edmund Kara's sculpture in wood of the Phoenix bird, a figure representative of the name Nepenthe.
(Lewis Josselyn Photo — Pat Hathaway Collection)

Henry Miller arrived here in 1944 and first lived at Anderson Canyon. Later he settled high above the fog line on Partington Ridge. His under-the-counter books brought him notoriety and his devotees often traveled to Big Sur in search of a glimpse of this man who wrote so honestly and eloquently about life. More than any other resident, Miller brought worldwide recognition of the name Big Sur. Even today, a decade after his death, people still ask where Henry Miller lives.

In his 1957 book *Big Sur and the Oranges of Hieronymus Bosch*, Miller writes of his Big Sur neighbors: *I have talked of Big Sur as if it were a place apart, having little or no connection with the world. Nothing could be less true. Nowhere else in my travels have I found individuals more alert to what is going on in the world, or better informed. It is rare that a community so small as this can boast so many world travelers. Nearly all of the women are excellent cooks, and the men as well oftentimes. Every other home possesses a connoiseur of wines; and every other father has the makings of an excellent mother. Never have I known a community in which there was so much talent, so many capable men and women, so many resourceful, self-sufficient souls.*

In May of 1944, Orson Welles purchased the Trails Club log cabin for around $15,000, supposedly, as a hideaway for Rita Hayworth, his wife of a short time. In 1947, Bill and Lolly Fassett bought the property from Welles and began creating what would become a Big Sur institution—the celebrated Nepenthe Restaurant. Rowan Maiden, a former apprentice of Frank Lloyd Wright, designed the structure which also exemplifies the expert craftsmanship of the area's finest builders.

In 1949, the Fassetts and their five children officially opened the restaurant and began serving the still famous Ambrosia burgers. Many visitors and residents cherish memories of unforgettable evenings spent dancing on Nepenthe's terrace with its stunning views of the south coast and Big Sur hills.

Power lines reached Big Sur in 1949. By 1951, most residents along the highway were using electricity. In 1956, residents started using telephones with their own dial service. Today, some residents of the remote south coast continue to live without electricity and telephones.

In 1948, residents complained that Big Sur was becoming too crowded. This same grievance had been expressed in the early 1900's and would be repeated in the '60's, '70's and '80's.

Eric Barker, another well known poet of the coast, settled here in the early 1950's. His verse characterized the Sur country's inspirational elements. Barker's poetry attracted the literary world's attention in 1956 when it was recognized for several awards. The following poem expresses his love for this country:

Big Sur
I loose faith in words in this country,
Better to leave unsaid
The poems that cannot describe the highest arcs
Of turning and turning hawks, the mountainous
Voyaging leisure of animal-changing clouds.
What words released from this granite shoulder
Can return like a cliff-falling gull
Translating a mood of the sea?
Or striking such wild notes as two hawks now
Down-circling their hazardous air?
Better let the truth be spoken
By what inhabits here from birth:
The autochthonous voice
Interpreting its own environment.
Better to stand and listen
To sounds not alien here.

The Big Sur Potluck Revue originated in 1952 and became an annual event. The local talent production continues to delight audiences, usually in the spring of the year. The Revue and other Big Sur events are held at the Grange hall, built by residents in the early 1950's.

In 1959 a group of Big Sur residents came together to prepare a plan to protect the scenic values of Big Sur. Among the original designers of this innovative proposal were planning expert Keith Evans, the late diplomat Nicholas Roosevelt, and the late architect Nathaniel Owings. These Big Sur residents, like those who preceded them and those who followed, recognized Big Sur's need for special attention if the virgin qualities of the landscape and coastline were to be preserved.

Their original conceptions became the Big Sur Master Plan. In 1961, it was approved and adopted by Monterey County. The plan was the first of its kind designed for the protection of scenic values and it became a model for the rest of the nation. Following this, the state legislature resolved that Highway One through Big Sur would forever remain a two lane, rural road.

In 1964 the film *the sandpiper* was filmed in Big Sur. Many believe this film, starring Elizabeth Taylor and Richard Burton had a pronounced effect on the coming of the hippies in the mid-sixties. The film portrayed free wheeling artists in a loose and carefree lifestyle in Big Sur.

In the fifties they were called "beatniks." Later, folks were calling them what they called themselves—"hippies." Until 1970 these itinerants continued to move into Big Sur, frustrating the residents by camping on their land, starting fires, being overbearing, and violating the rights of others.

Requests were made by the local residents to county officials for help in curbing this situation. Often when a resident asked one of these unwanted "immigrants" to leave his land or to put out a fire, he was told that it wasn't his (the resident's) land; it was God's land for all to enjoy.

By the early seventies the social revolution of the hippies had ended, and today many of these once unkempt rebels of society live average American lifestyles.

In 1972, Andrew Molera State Park on the northern end of the Big Sur Valley opened as a walk-in campground.

On August 1, 1972, a forest fire began on the west side of Highway 1, just north of the Big Sur village. It was set by a camper at the newly opened Andrew Molera State Park. Sweeping northeastward to the top of the main ridge and south along the east side of the valley, the fire burned for six days, and cost $850,000 to contain. In the end, 4,300 acres of land above the east side of the valley were burned.

The most dangerous result of the fire was the burning of several watershed tributaries—Pfeiffer-Redwood Creek in the State Park, Juan Higuera Creek, which runs beside the Big Sur Grange, and Phenegar Creek, which runs beside the old River Village and River Inn buildings.

When plant cover is burned off, the ground and soil become vulnerable to rainfall. As a result, runoff such as mud may slide down the mountainous slopes to the valley below.

In mid-October and mid-November 1972, heavy rains came to Big Sur and before it was all over the entire River Village, including Dick and Pat Hartford's Village Store, the post office, garage, Kay Short's real estate office and several trailers were destroyed by walls of mud, moving rocks and trees. The mudslides roared through the Pfeiffer-Big Sur State Park and caused extensive damage. Further south Gary Koeppel's Coast Gallery was extensively damaged and the highway there was washed out. A highway worker clearing mud from the road was killed when the mud came down suddenly and swept him over the side.

Disaster had come to Big Sur. A number of cars were swept away and little compensation was waiting for the victims. The insurance companies called the disaster "an act of God," and therefore did not cover damages. Most of the victims suffered extensive financial loss.

After the heavy rains and mudslides of the winter of 1972, scenes such as this were not uncommon along the lower reaches of the Big Sur River. This house trailer owned by the River Inn was buried six feet when great walls of mud came down the mountain slope destroying everything in its path. This particular disaster was the direct result of a forest fire set by a camper at the newly opened Andrew Molera State Park in August, 1972. The fire burned the majority of the watershed of three major creek drainages in the Big Sur Valley; without the ground cover to hold soil together, it slides down the steep slopes when heavy rains occur.

The Marble-Cone Fire, second largest in the history of California, burned out of control for three weeks in the high country of Big Sur. Not only did the fire devastate the lives of thousands of animals, birds and fish in the wilderness, it burned the majority of the watershed that runs off through the Big Sur River. This brought the threat of heavy flooding in the Big Sur Valley upon arrival of the heavy winter rains.
(Monterey Peninsula Herald Russ Cain Photo)

Pat and Dick Hartford owned and operated the Village Store for seventeen years. Not only did they lose their business in the slides but their home as well. The Hartfords left Big Sur and opened a new resort business in northern California, just one mile south of Garberville. It's called *The Benbow Village Green.* Big Sur people miss the Hartford's and their Village Store.

In August 1977, the Marble Cone Fire burned almost 200,000 acres of the Ventana Wilderness east of Big Sur. It burned for nearly a month and destroyed ninety percent of the vegetation cover in the upper Big Sur watershed, creating the danger of serious flooding, particularly through the channel of the Big Sur River.

Rainfall from January through May of 1978 amounted to sixty-seven inches but brought no major disaster to Big Sur. Millions of dollars were spent by the state to prevent a recurrence of the 1972 mudslides.

In the 1970's, tourism was on the upsurge in Big Sur. Outsiders publicly discussed "saving" Big Sur. Some offered ideas such as making the entire coast a federal park.

In 1978 residents discussed the incorporation of Big Sur. Incorporation would officially designate the rural community as an actual town, with its own government.

In October, 1978 the Big Sur Historical Society was formed. The first meeting, held at the State Park Lodge on the original site of Pfeiffer's Resort, featured Esther Ewoldsen, the charming daughter of the late John Pfeiffer. Mrs. Ewoldsen told interesting and amusing stories of early life in Big Sur and at the family's resort.

NATURE ❧
The Supreme Attraction

*T*he air, water, soil and living things are abundant and forceful in Big Sur. Hundreds of species of plants and animals live in the mountains, on the rocky shoreline, and in the redwood forests near the Big and Little Sur Rivers.

One need not know a lot about this "world apart" for man to enjoy it, for it is free for the taking. And as we all know, the best things in life are free! Let your senses come alive to the beauty around you. No cinematographer in the world can even come close to matching the lovely display of color and soul-stirring inspiration which nature so gratuitously provides.

What Used To Be:

Prior to the 1880's, the **grizzly bear** was plentiful in the Santa Lucia Mountains of Big Sur. They no longer exist, although occasionally a hiker will claim to have seen one. In the winter of 1978, sightings of **black bears** were reported in the southernmost wilderness region.

The once plentiful **mountain lion** has been hunted out of the back country. Some still roam the hills, but it is a protected species and cannot be hunted. They are usually fearful of man, but do kill livestock and smaller animals.

We are all inspired when nature stages a lavish sunset display. Along the Big Sur coast spectacular sunsets are not uncommon, especially when clouds are present and give the last rays of the day's sun infinite changes in color, form and shading. Shorebirds crowd the rocky coastline for its abundant nesting sites and the availability of fish, but one has to wonder if these little fellas don't stay around the coast just for its panoramic sunsets. (Photo by Larry French)

Tall columns of redwood trees rise from the forest in Big Sur. The ancestry of the coast redwood (Sequoia semper-virens) goes back millions of years; some of the trees themselves are thousands of years old. You may find yourself looking at a redwood tree that was growing at the time of Christ. Age, size and beauty have qualified the redwoods as the most famous of all trees. Coast redwoods, one of the two remaining species, are found intermittently along the California coast as far south as Salmon Creek on the southern Big Sur coastline in Monterey County. Coast redwoods also grow on the extreme southern coast of Oregon and might be found growing inland from the coast as far as thirty-five miles. (Photo by Thomas Gundelfinger)

The Abundant Species:

More species of birds live in this section of the coastal area than any other location in California. A **golden eagle** is occasionally spotted. The **red-tailed hawk** is a graceful sight as he soars in and out of canyons. **Stellar's jay** is a deep blue, fussy bird with a crest atop its head. This bird is prevalent in the area, along with the **belted kingfisher** which rarely misses its target when diving for fish in the river. The tiny, colorful **hummingbird** is fun to watch in its stationary position in mid-air as it feeds on the nectar of flowers in the summer. One of the most attractive of the birds is the female **California quail** whose fine-looking plumage curves forward from her head. Many species of shorebirds can be seen around the beaches, including **western gulls, cormorants,** and **pelicans.**

Plant Life

The botanical resources of Big Sur are overwhelming to the senses. Wildflowers bloom in the spring and throughout much of the summer, carpeting the ground with a potpourri of colors that complement an already breathtaking landscape. Among the most prevalent of the wildflowers visible from the Coast Highway are the delicate orange **California poppy**, the white, blue, yellow, and purple forms of **lupine**, the orange **bush monkey flowers**, and the reddish-orange **Indian paintbrush.** Herbs and spices of many varieties grow wild in Big Sur, and the abundant display of yellow that you notice on the sides of the highway and hillsides is probably **wild mustard.**

Numerous species of ferns grow in the canyons and on the banks of creeks and the two rivers. The **western bracken, sword fern, five-finger, maiden hair,** and **licorice fern** are but a few.

The coastline, canyons, river banks, and higher elevations support particular types of trees, due to differences in climate.

Along the banks of the Big Sur River one finds **alder, sycamore**, and the ever-present **redwood**. The **big leaf maple, California laurel (or bay), eucalyptus, madrone,** and several variety of **pines** are located throughout the area.

At the higher elevations of the Santa Lucia Mountains a number of trees are found which also grow in the Sierra Nevada at similar altitudes. Among the endemics to the area, the **Monterey cypress**, can be seen growing at many locations from the highway. The famous **Santa Lucia fir**, is found scattered throughout the upper reaches of the mountains. This famous tall, symmetrical tree is found nowhere else in the world and has no known near relative. Very few of these trees exist.

The **coast redwood** is one of the two remaining species of redwoods. The coast redwood grows on the western coast while the other known species, the sierra redwood grows in the interior mountains of California.

The coast redwood grows along the entire length of the Big Sur coast and makes its last stand on the North American continent at Salmon Creek on the southern coast. It grows only within the existence of the summer fog belt, but may extend inland as far as twenty to thirty miles.

The redwoods are the oldest of all trees, their ancestry going back for millions of years. Among other "claims to fame," they are also the largest, tallest and perhaps most famous of all trees. They may grow as high as 350 feet and the diameter of mature trees ranges from twelve to sixteen feet. The age of mature trees is from 800 to 1,500 years. The maximum reported age of a coast redwood is 2,000 years. It is said that as many as twenty average sized houses could be built from a large tree.

The bark is dull red to dark brown in color and heavily ridged. Its thickness is from thee inches to one foot at the base of the huge tree.

The Save the Redwoods League is a California organization concerned with the preservation of these unique "living fossils."

Furry Critters and the Like

The migration of the **California gray whale** up and down the California coast is a bi-annual event. The mild-mannered, intelligent whales travel south along the coast from Arctic waters where they have been feeding on the nourishing plant and animal life of the Bering Sea. This southward migration to the Baja California lagoons on the west coast of Mexico is made during the months of November, December and January with a few stragglers following shortly thereafter. At this time the playful whales can be seen just off the coast, spouting when they surface, every three or four minutes for breathing. Quite often when the male leaps from the water he is trying to get the romantic attention of a female.

While enroute to Mexico where they will breed and give birth to their calves, about half of the females are heavy with "child" and are allowed to lead the journey, followed by the unmated females, the males, and finally by the young calves.

With mating and calving accomplished in the Mexican lagoons, the whales begin the northward migration back to Arctic waters. This return trip is not as easy to observe since it is a more rushed journey and they often travel further offshore. It is thought that as many as 12,000 of these forty-to-fifty foot mammals travel the 7,000 mile one-way migration route each year.

Raccoons seem to be non-existent during daylight hours, but when the sun goes down the little nocturnal animals come out in abundant numbers. Zealous meat eaters, they sneak into the campgrounds at night and actually manage to break into locked ice chests and take the food so expertly that they are seldomly caught in the act. They have earned the name "Little Bandit."

Brown, gray, and black in color, the raccoon's face is actually covered with a black mask, and its long tail is marked with black rings. They keep their distance from people as a rule, except perhaps when food is being offered.

Because the raccoon washes everything he eats, it is thought that he has a salivary deficiency and needs the excess wetness in order to chew the food. One thing is certain; where there is food and darkness, there will also be raccoons.

Raccoon raids are unavoidable for the campers and mountain dwellers in Big Sur. Prowling raccoons (Procyon lotor) *come out each night in abundant numbers in search of food, often breaking into the locked ice chests of campers, making very little noise in the process. The black masklike facial markings of the little furry critter further substantiates his well earned nickname, "Little Bandit."* (Photo by Paula Walling)

The **wild boar** (European wild pig) was introduced to the Santa Lucia Mountains of Big Sur after being imported from Europe by hunting enthusiasts in the 1920's. These animals are frightful looking, to say the least, with long naked snouts and a pair of razor sharp tusks that extend from the sides of the snout and measure up to seven inches in length. These burly animals grow to four to five feet in length and weigh as much as 600 pounds. They are dark gray to black in color and their hair is stiff and coarse.

Preferring dusk and darkness, they come out at night to dig in the ground for roots. Folks living on the mountains in Big Sur have on occasion awakened to find their lawns and gardens plowed by these hungry nocturnal creatures. Boars are normally shy and choose to avoid man unless a sow feels that her piglets are in danger.

The gestation period for the boar is only four months with as many as a dozen piglets produced in one litter. Most sows produce two such litters a year.

While they are rarely seen because of their nocturnal habits, the first rain of a season may bring them out in daylight because the ground is soft and easy to dig for roots.

For over a century the good-natured **sea otter** was thought to be extinct after extensive killing by hunters for the valuable furs. In 1938, however, they were observed on the Big Sur coast, which today is a sea otter refuge protected by law.

The adorable sea otters live in the profuse kelp beds (kelp is a coarse, brown seaweed that grows extensively on rocky coasts) which supply the playful creatures with food and refuge. Their lifestyle makes one somewhat envious as it is comprised mainly of eating, sleeping, playing and making love. Their diet is one that we humans could not afford, since the gourmet's delight of **abalone** is one of the most popular of the protein-rich shellfish and seafood that the otters eat. Their furry coats keep them warm as well as serving as pockets where they sometimes store food in the loose skin under their arms.

This member of the weasel family is from four to five feet in length and may weigh from sixty to eighty-five pounds, the female being somewhat smaller than the male. The fat-faced, bewhiskered otters breathe air. They are excellent swimmers and divers. Sleeping and relaxing is done while lying on their backs in the water, and quite often they are seen eating in this position with food resting on their stomachs.

The **black-tailed deer** is quite populous in the area. They are easily distinguished by their black tails. They move around quite a bit in search of food and warm temperatures, and may be seen on the Coast Highway at night and in early morning.

The deer's average life span is ten years. The deer herds in Big Sur seem to be increasing and are in no danger of extinction.

The southern sea otter (Enhydra lutris nereis) *lives along the entire length of the Big Sur coast, but is best observed just offshore in the kelp beds at Soberanes Point, Julia Pfeiffer-Burns State Park, Big Creek, Limekiln Beach, Kirk Creek and Alder Creek. Swimming belly-up, the otter holds his forepaws across his chest, often along with shellfish or kelp he is eating. In the loose fold of skin under his arm, he often stores food or carries a rock that is used for cracking shellfish. Once thought to be near extinction, the population growth of these adorable marine mammals is slow and estimated at around 1500.* Friends of the Sea Otter *is a non-profit organization formed to aid in the protection and maintenace of a healthy otter population along the California Coast.* (Photo by Ralph Fairfield)

A multitude of other interesting mammals inhabit the land and sea of Big Sur. Among them are the **coyote, ringtail cat, sea lion** and **harbor seal.**

The black-tail deer of Big Sur live in the forest above 1000 feet but they are often seen along the highway and near the beaches at night and in early morning. In the forest they spend their days resting in the thickets, and move around in the late afternoon and evening in search of food and temperatures. The antlers of the bucks are shed in the late autumn after the rutting season of mating.
(Photo by Carlton Shadwell)

A full moon over Big Sur enhances an already melodramatic setting of mountains and rolling hills beside the vast ocean, giving the usually dark night the appearance of twilight. (Photo by Carlton Shadwell)

Helpful things to know about Big Sur

Big Sur Health Center • Located just inside the entrance to the Big Sur Campground. Open Monday, Wednesday and Friday. Telephone (408) 667-2580

Big Sur Library • Located next to Ripplewood Resort. Telephone (408) 667-2537

Big Sur Post Office • Located next to the Big Sur Center Deli & Bazaar on Highway 1, 1.7 miles south of the Pfieffer-Big Sur State Park entrance. Telephone (408) 667-2305

Point Sur Lighthouse Tours • Given each Sunday. Telephone (408) 625-4419

Monterey Peninsula Transit • Four daily round trips from Big Sur to Carmel-Monterey area, from late April to early October. Telephone (408) 899-2555

Monterey Peninsula Airport • From Big Sur, travel north on Highway 1 for thirty miles to the Salinas-Highway 68 exit. Go east for about two miles & follow the signs to the airport.

Real Estate Representatives -

• Fox and Carskadon. Robert Cross, Realtor. P.O. Box 244, Big Sur, CA 93920. Telephone (408) 667-2222

• Heinrich, Dusenbury and Associates. Hank Adams, Linda Mazet or Jean Mason. P.O. Box 222318, Carmel, CA 93922. (408) 625-6225

Nearby Places of Interest

Monterey Bay Aquarium • On historic Cannery Row. Daily tours. Telephone (408) 375-3333

Hearst Castle • A two hour, 60 mile drive from the Big Sur Valley. Daily tours. Telephone (805) 927-2000

Photographing Big Sur

• A polarizing filter on your 35 mm camera lens reduces glare and atmospheric haze, and enhances the color of your slides and prints.

• For best results when photographing land and seascapes: Aim your camera northward from early morning to midday, and south in the afternoon. As a general rule in the northern hemisphere, the bluest skies are photographed shooting north.

• Photograph the forest and redwoods when the sun is high, and filtering through the trees.

59

About the Author

Born and raised in Anderson, South Carolina, Tomi Lussier traveled west to California after college. She was attracted to Big Sur by its magic and inspiration and what began as mere infatuation with this tip-tilted land soon blossomed into a full blown love affair. She continues to live, love, and work at her home on the southern edge of the Big Sur Valley.

To The Reader

I hope that after you have read and examined this book, you'll write me your reactions, offer suggestions, make corrections, or tell me something that you know and I don't. These pages are for you, the reader, and my ultimate wish is that this be a true and accurate guide about Big Sur.

Tomi Lussier
P.O. Box 340
Big Sur, CA 93920

Point Sur Rock with lighthouse atop. Rarely seen view of the point looking northward. Highway One snakes its way north along the coast towards, the Monterey Peninsula, some twenty miles away.

BIG SUR PUBLICATIONS